HBR Guide to
Data Analytics Basics for Managers

Harvard Business Review Guides

Arm yourself with the advice you need to succeed on the job, from the most trusted brand in business. Packed with how-to essentials from leading experts, the HBR Guides provide smart answers to your most pressing work challenges.

The titles include:

HBR Guide to Being More Productive

HBR Guide to Better Business Writing

HBR Guide to Building Your Business Case

HBR Guide to Buying a Small Business

HBR Guide to Coaching Employees

HBR Guide to Data Analytics Basics for Managers

HBR Guide to Delivering Effective Feedback

HBR Guide to Emotional Intelligence

HBR Guide to Finance Basics for Managers

HBR Guide to Getting the Right Work Done

HBR Guide to Leading Teams

HBR Guide to Making Every Meeting Matter

HBR Guide to Managing Stress at Work

HBR Guide to Managing Up and Across

HBR Guide to Negotiating

HBR Guide to Office Politics

HBR Guide to Performance Management

HBR Guide to Persuasive Presentations

HBR Guide to Project Management

HBR Guide to
Data Analytics Basics for Managers

HARVARD BUSINESS REVIEW PRESS

Boston, Massachusetts

Copyright 2018 Harvard Business School Publishing Corporation

10 9 8 7 6 5 4 3 2 1

The web addresses referenced in this book were live and correct at the time of the book's publication but may be subject to change.

Cataloging-in-Publication data is forthcoming

ISBN: 978-1-63369-557-3

What You'll Learn

The vast amounts of data that companies accumulate today can help you understand the past, make predictions about the future, and guide your decision making. But how do you use all this data effectively? How do you assess whether your findings are accurate or significant? How do you distinguish between causation and correlation? And how do you present your results in a way that will persuade others?

Understanding data analytics is an essential skill for every manager. It's no longer enough to hand this responsibility off to data experts. To be able to rely on the evidence your analysts give you, you need to know where it comes from and how it was generated—and what it can and can't teach you.

Using quantitative analysis as part of your decision making helps you uncover new information and provides you with more confidence in your choices—and you don't need to be deeply proficient in statistics to do it. This guide gives you the basics so you can better understand how to use data and analytics as you make tough choices in your daily work. It walks you through three fundamental steps of data analysis: gathering the information you need, making sense of the numbers, and communicating those findings to get buy-in and spur others to action.

You'll learn to:

- Ask the right questions to get the information you need

- Work more effectively with data scientists

- Run business experiments and A/B tests

- Choose the right metrics to evaluate predictions and performance

- Assess whether you can trust your data

- Understand the basics of regression analysis and statistical significance

- Distinguish between correlation and causation

- Sidestep cognitive biases when making decisions

- Identify when to invest in machine learning—and how to proceed

- Communicate and defend your findings to stakeholders

- Visualize your data clearly and powerfully

Contents

Contents

SECTION THREE

Analyze the Data

SECTION FOUR

Communicate Your Findings

Contents

Introduction

Data is coming into companies at remarkable speed and volume. From small, manageable data sets to big data that is recorded every time a consumer buys a product or likes a social media post, this information offers a range of opportunities to managers.

Data allows you to make better predictions about the future—whether a new retail location is likely to succeed, for example, or what a reasonable budget for the next fiscal year might look like. It helps you identify the causes of certain events—a failed advertising campaign, a bad quarter, or even poor employee performance—so you can adjust course if necessary. It allows you to isolate variables so that you can identify your customers' wants or needs or assess the chances an initiative will succeed. Data gives you insight on factors affecting your industry or marketplace and can inform your decisions about anything from new product development to hiring choices.

But with so much information coming in, how do you sort through it all and make sense of everything? It's tempting to hand that role off to your experts and analysts. But even if you have the brightest minds handling your data, it won't make a difference if you don't know what they're doing or what it means. Unless you know how to use that data to inform your decisions, all you have is a set of numbers.

It's quickly becoming a requirement that every decision maker have a basic understanding of data analytics. But if the thought of statistical analysis makes you sweat, have no fear. You don't need to become a data scientist or statistician to understand what the numbers mean (even if data scientists have the "sexiest job of the 21st century"—see the bonus article we've included in the appendix). Instead, you as a manager need a clear understanding of how these experts reach their results and how to best use that information to guide your own decisions. You must know where their findings come from, ask the right questions of data sets, and translate the results to your colleagues and other stakeholders in a way that convinces and persuades.

This book is not for analytics experts—the data scientists, analysts, and other specialists who do this work day in, day out. Instead, it's meant for managers who may not have a background in statistical analysis but still want to improve their decisions using data. This book will not give you a detailed course in statistics. Rather, it will help you better *use* data, so you can understand what the numbers are telling you, identify where the results of those calculations may be falling short, and make stronger choices about how to run your business.

What This Book Will Do

This guide walks you through three key areas of the data analytics process: gathering the information you need, analyzing it, and communicating your findings to others. These three steps form the core of managerial data analytics.

To fully understand these steps, you need to see the process of data analytics and your role within it at a high level. Section 1, "Getting Started," provides two pieces to help you digest the process from start to finish. First, Thomas Davenport outlines your role in data analysis and describes how you can work more effectively with your data scientist and become a better consumer of analytics. Then, you'll find an easy exercise you can do yourself to gather your own data, analyze it, and identify what to do next in light of what you've discovered.

Once you have this basic understanding of the process, you can move on to learn the specifics about each step, starting with the data search.

Gather the right information

For any analysis, you need data—that's obvious. But what data you need and how to get it can be less clear and can vary, depending on the problem to be solved. Section 2 begins by providing a list of questions to ask for a targeted data search.

There are two ways to get the information you need: by asking others for existing data and analysis or by running your own experiment to gather new data. We explore both of these approaches in turn, covering how to request information from your data experts (taking into account their needs and concerns) and using the scientific method and A/B testing for well-thought-out tests.

But any data search won't matter if you don't measure useful things. Defining the right metrics ensures that your results align with your needs. Jeff Bladt, chief data officer at DoSomething.org, and Bob Filbin, chief data scientist at Crisis Text Line, use the example of their own social media campaign to explain how to identify and work toward metrics that matter.

We end this section with a helpful process by data expert and company adviser Thomas C. Redman. Before you can move forward with any analysis, you must know if the information you have can be trusted. By following his advice, you can assess the quality of your data, make corrections as necessary, and move forward accordingly, even if the data isn't perfect.

Analyze the data

You have the numbers—now what? It's usually at this point in the process that managers flash back to their college statistics courses and nervously leave the analysis to an expert or a computer algorithm. Certainly, the data scientists on your team are there to help. But you can learn the basics of analysis without needing to understand every mathematical calculation. By focusing on how data experts and companies *use* these equations (instead of how they run them), we help you ask the right questions and inform your decisions in real-world managerial situations.

We begin section 3 by describing some basic terms and processes. We define predictive analytics and how to use them, and explain statistical concepts like regression analysis, correlation versus causation, and statistical significance. You'll also learn how to assess if machine learning can help solve your problem—and how to proceed if it does.

In this section, we also aim to help you avoid common traps as you study data and make decisions. You'll discover how to look at numbers in nonlinear ways, so your predictions are more accurate. And you will find practical ways to avoid injecting subconscious bias into your choices.

Finally, recognize when the story you're being told may be too good to be true. Even with the best data—and the best data analysts—the results may not be as clear as you think. As Michael Schrage, research fellow at MIT's Sloan School Center for Digital Business, points out in the last piece in this section, an unmentioned outlier can throw an entire conclusion off base, which is a risk you can't take with your decision making.

Communicate your findings

"Never make the mistake of assuming that the results will 'speak for themselves,'" warns Thomas Davenport in the final section of this book. You must know how to communicate the results of your analysis and use that information to persuade others and drive your decision forward—the third step in the data analytics process.

Section 4 explains how to share data with others so that the numbers support your message, rather than distract from it. The next few chapters outline when visualizations will be helpful to your data—and when they won't be—as well as the basics of making persuasive charts. You'll learn how to depict and explain the uncertainty and the probability of events, as well as what to do if someone questions your findings.

Data alone will not elicit change, though; you must use this evidence in the right way to inform and change the mindset of the person who sees it. Data is merely supporting material, says presentations expert Nick Morgan in the final chapter. To truly persuade, you need a story with emotional power.

Set your organization up for success

While we hope that you'll continue to learn and grow your own analytical skills, it's likely that you'll continue to work with data experts and quants throughout your data journey. Understanding the role of the data scientist will be crucial to ensuring your organization has the capabilities it needs to grow through data.

Data scientists bring with them intense curiosity and make new discoveries that managers and analysts may not see themselves. As an appendix at the end of this book, you'll find Thomas H. Davenport and D.J. Patil's popular article "Data Scientist: The Sexiest Job of the 21st Century." Davenport and Patil's piece aims to help you better understand this key player in an organization—someone they describe as a "hybrid of data hacker, analyst, communicator, and trusted adviser." These individuals have rare qualities that, as a manager, you may not fully understand. By reading through this piece, you'll have insight into how they think about and work with data. What's more, you'll learn how to find, attract, and develop data scientists to keep your company on the competing edge.

Moving Forward

Data-driven decisions won't come easily. But by understanding the basics of data analytics, you'll be able to ask the right questions of data to pull the most useful information out of the numbers. Before diving in to the chapters that follow, though, ask yourself how often you're incorporating data into your daily work. The assessment "Are You Data Driven?" is a brief test that will help you target your efforts. With that knowledge in mind, move through the next sections with an open mind, ready to weave data into each of your decisions.

ARE YOU DATA DRIVEN?

by Thomas C. Redman

Look at the list below and give yourself a point for every behavior you demonstrate consistently and half a point for those you follow most—but not all—of the time. Be hard on yourself. If you can only cite an instance or two, don't give yourself any credit.

☐ I push decisions down to the lowest possible level.

☐ I bring as much diverse data and as many diverse viewpoints to any situation as I possibly can.

(continued)

ARE YOU DATA DRIVEN?

(continued)

☐ I use data to develop a deeper understanding of the business context and the problem at hand.

☐ I develop an appreciation for variation.

☐ I deal reasonably well with uncertainty.

☐ I integrate my understanding of the data and its implications with my intuition.

☐ I recognize the importance of high-quality data and invest to make improvements.

☐ I conduct experiments and research to supplement existing data and address new questions.

☐ I recognize that decision criteria can vary with circumstances.

☐ I realize that making a decision is only the first step, and I revise decisions as new data comes to light.

☐ I work to learn new skills, and bring new data and data technologies into my organization.

☐ I learn from my mistakes and help others to do so as well.

☐ I strive to be a role model when it comes to data, and work with leaders, peers, and subordinates to help them become data driven.

Tally your points. If you score less than 7, it's imperative that you start changing the way you work as soon as possible. Target those behaviors where you gave yourself partial credit first and fully embed those skills into your daily work. Then build on your success by targeting those behaviors that you were unable to give yourself any credit for. It may help to enlist a colleague's aid—the two of you can improve together.

If you score a 7 or higher, you're showing signs of being data driven. Still, strive for ongoing improvement. Set a goal of learning a new behavior or two every year. Take this test every six months to make sure that you're on track.

Adapted from "Are You Data Driven? Take a Hard Look in the Mirror" on hbr.org, July 11, 2013 (product # H00AX2).

Thomas C. Redman, "the Data Doc," is President of Data Quality Solutions. He helps companies and people, including startups, multinationals, executives, and leaders at all levels, chart their courses to data-driven futures. He places special emphasis on quality, analytics, and organizational capabilities.

SECTION ONE

Getting Started

CHAPTER 1

Keep Up with Your Quants

by Thomas H. Davenport

"I don't know why we didn't get the mortgages off our books," a senior quantitative analyst at a large U.S. bank told me a few years ago. "I had a model strongly indicating that a lot of them wouldn't be repaid, and I sent it to the head of our mortgage business."

When I asked the leader of the mortgage business why he'd ignored the advice, he said, "If the analyst showed me a model, it wasn't in terms I could make sense of. I didn't even know his group was working on repayment probabilities." The bank ended up losing billions in bad loans.

We live in an era of big data. Whether you work in financial services, consumer goods, travel and transpor-

Reprinted from *Harvard Business Review*, July–August 2013 (product #R1307L).

tation, or industrial products, analytics are becoming a competitive necessity for your organization. But as the banking example shows, having big data—and even people who can manipulate it successfully—is not enough. Companies need general managers who can partner effectively with "quants" to ensure that their work yields better strategic and tactical decisions.

For people fluent in analytics—such as Gary Loveman of Caesars Entertainment (with a PhD from MIT), Jeff Bezos of Amazon (an electrical engineering and computer science major from Princeton), or Sergey Brin and Larry Page of Google (computer science PhD dropouts from Stanford)—there's no problem. But if you're a typical executive, your math and statistics background probably amounts to a college class or two. You might be adept at using spreadsheets and know your way around a bar graph or a pie chart, but when it comes to analytics, you often feel quantitatively challenged.

So what does the shift toward data-driven decision making mean for you? How do you avoid the fate of the loss-making mortgage bank head and instead lead your company into the analytical revolution, or at least become a good foot soldier in it? This article—a primer for non-quants—is based on extensive interviews with executives, including some with whom I've worked as a teacher or a consultant.

You, the Consumer

Start by thinking of yourself as a consumer of analytics. The producers are the quants whose analyses and models you'll integrate with your business experience and intuition as you make decisions. Producers are, of course, good at gathering the available data and making predictions about the future. But most lack sufficient knowledge to identify hypotheses and relevant variables and to know when the ground beneath an organization is shifting. Your job as a data consumer—to generate hypotheses and determine whether results and recommendations make sense in a changing business environment—is therefore critically important. That means accepting a few key responsibilities. Some require only changes in attitude and perspective; others demand a bit of study.

Learn a little about analytics

If you remember the content of your college-level statistics course, you may be fine. If not, bone up on the basics of regression analysis, statistical inference, and experimental design. You need to understand the process for making analytical decisions, including when you should step in as a consumer, and you must recognize that every analytical model is built on assumptions that producers ought to explain and defend. (See the sidebar "Analytics-Based Decision Making—in Six Steps.") As the famous statistician George Box noted, "All models are wrong, but some are useful." In other words, models intentionally simplify our complex world.

To become more data literate, enroll in an executive education program in statistics, take an online course, or learn from the quants in your organization by working closely with them on one or more projects.

Jennifer Joy, the vice president of clinical operations at Cigna, took the third approach. Joy has a nursing

ANALYTICS-BASED DECISION MAKING—IN SIX KEY STEPS

When using big data to make big decisions, non-quants should focus on the first and the last steps of the process. The numbers people typically handle the details in the middle, but wise non-quants ask lots of questions along the way.

1. *Recognize the problem or question.* Frame the decision or business problem, and identify possible alternatives to the framing.

2. *Review previous findings.* Identify people who have tried to solve this problem or similar ones—and the approaches they used.

3. *Model the solution and select the variables.* Formulate a detailed hypothesis about how particular variables affect the outcome.

4. *Collect the data.* Gather primary and secondary data on the hypothesized variables.

5. *Analyze the data.* Run a statistical model, assess its appropriateness for the data, and repeat the process until a good fit is found.

6. *Present and act on the results.* Use the data to tell a story to decision makers and stakeholders so that they will take action.

degree and an MBA, but she wasn't entirely comfortable with her analytical skills. She knew, however, that the voluminous reports she received about her call center operations weren't telling her whether the coaching calls made to patients were actually helping to manage their diseases and to keep them out of the hospital.

So Joy reached out to Cigna's analytics group, in particular to the experts on experimental design—the only analytical approach that can potentially demonstrate cause and effect. She learned, for example, that she could conduct pilot studies to discover which segments of her targeted population benefit the most (and which the least) from her call center's services. Specifically, she uses analytics to "prematch" pairs of patients and then to randomly assign one member of the pair to receive those services, while the other gets an alternative such as a mail-order or an online-support intervention. Each pilot lasts just a couple of months, and multiple studies are run simultaneously—so Joy now gets information about the effectiveness of her programs on a rolling basis.

In the end, Joy and her quant partners learned that the coaching worked for people with certain diseases but not for other patients, and some call center staff members were redeployed as a result. Now her group regularly conducts 20 to 30 such tests a year to find out what really makes a difference for patients. She may not understand all the methodological details, but as Michael Cousins, the vice president of U.S. research and analytics at Cigna, attests, she's learned to be "very analytically oriented."

Align yourself with the right kind of quant

Karl Kempf, a leader in Intel's decision-engineering group, is known at the company as the "überquant" or "chief mathematician." He often says that effective quantitative decisions "are not about the math; they're about the relationships." What he means is that quants and the consumers of their data get much better results if they form deep, trusting ties that allow them to exchange information and ideas freely.

Of course, highly analytical people are not always known for their social skills, so this can be hard work. As one wag jokingly advised, "Look for the quants who stare at your shoes, instead of their own, when you engage them in conversation." But it's possible to find people who communicate well and have a passion for solving business—rather than mathematical—problems and, after you've established a relationship, to encourage frank dialogue and data-driven dissent between the two of you.

Katy Knox, at Bank of America, has learned how to align with data producers. As the head of retail strategy and distribution for the bank's consumer division, she oversees 5,400-plus branches serving more than 50 million consumers and small businesses. For several years she's been pushing her direct reports to use analytics to make better decisions—for example, about which branches to open or close, how to reduce customer wait times, what incentives lead to multichannel interactions, and why some salespeople are more productive than others.

Bank of America has hundreds of quants, but most of them were pooled in a group that managers could not easily access. Knox insisted on having her own analytics team, and she established a strong working relationship with its members through frequent meetings and project-reporting sessions. She worked especially closely with two team leaders, Justin Addis and Michael Hyzy, who have backgrounds in retail banking and Six Sigma, so they're able to understand her unit's business problems and communicate them to the hard-core quants they manage. After Knox set the precedent, Bank of America created a matrix structure for its analysts in the consumer bank, and most now report to both a business line and a centralized analytical group.

Focus on the beginning and the end

Framing a problem—identifying it and understanding how others might have solved it in the past—is the most important stage of the analytical process for a consumer of big data. It's where your business experience and intuition matter most. After all, a hypothesis is simply a hunch about how the world works. The difference with analytical thinking, of course, is that you use rigorous methods to test the hypothesis.

For example, executives at the two corporate parent organizations of Transitions Optical believed that the photochromic lens company might not be investing in marketing at optimal levels, but no empirical data confirmed or refuted that idea. Grady Lenski, who headed the marketing division at the time, decided to hire analytics consultants to measure the effectiveness of different sales campaigns—a constructive framing that expanded on the simple binary question of whether or not costs were too high.

If you're a non-quant, you should also focus on the final step in the process—presenting and communicating results to other executives—because it's one that many quants discount or overlook and that you'll probably have to take on yourself at some point. If analytics is largely about "telling a story with data," what type of story would you favor? What kind of language and tone would you use? Should the story be told in narrative or visual terms? What types of graphics do you like? No matter how sophisticated their analyses, quants should be encouraged to explain their results in a straightforward way so that everyone can understand—or you should do it for them. A statistical methods story ("first we ran a chi-square test, and then we converted the categorical data to ordinal, next we ran a logistic regression, and then we lagged the economic data by a year") is rarely acceptable.

Many businesspeople settle on an ROI story: How will the new decision-making model increase conversions, revenue, or profitability? For example, a Merck executive with responsibility for a global business unit has worked closely with the pharmaceutical company's commercial analytics group for many years to answer a variety of questions, including what the ROIs of direct-to-consumer promotions are. Before an ROI analysis, he and the group discuss what actions they will take when they find out whether promotions are highly, marginally, or not successful—to make clear that the effort isn't merely an academic exercise. After the analysis, the executive sits the analysts down at a table with his management team to present and debate the results.

Ask lots of questions along the way

Former U.S. Treasury Secretary Larry Summers, who once served as an adviser to a quantitative hedge fund, told me that his primary responsibility in that job was to "look over shoulders"—that is, to ask the smart quants in the firm equally smart questions about their models and assumptions. Many of them hadn't been pressed like that before; they needed an intelligent consumer of data to help them think through and improve their work.

No matter how much you trust your quants, don't stop asking them tough questions. Here are a few that almost always lead to more-rigorous, defensible analyses. (If you don't understand a reply, ask for one that uses simpler language.)

1. What was the source of your data?

2. How well do the sample data represent the population?

3. Does your data distribution include outliers? How did they affect the results?

4. What assumptions are behind your analysis? Might certain conditions render your assumptions and your model invalid?

5. Why did you decide on that particular analytical approach? What alternatives did you consider?

6. How likely is it that the independent variables are actually causing the changes in the dependent variable? Might other analyses establish causality more clearly?

Frank Friedman, the chief financial officer and managing partner for finance and administration of Deloitte's U.S. business, is an inveterate questioner. He has assembled a group of data scientists and quantitative analysts to help him with several initiatives, including optimizing the pricing of services, developing models that predict employee performance, and identifying factors that drive receivables. "People who work with me know I question a lot—everything—always," Friedman says. "After the questioning, they know they will have to go back and redo some of their analyses." He also believes it's vital to admit when you don't understand something: "I know I am not the smartest person in the room in my meetings with these people. I'm always pushing for greater clarity [because] if I can't articulate it, I can't defend it to others."

Establish a culture of inquiry, not advocacy

We all know how easily "figures lie and liars figure." Analytics consumers should never pressure their producers with comments like "See if you can find some evidence in the data to support my idea." Instead, your explicit goal should be to find the truth. As the head of Merck's commercial analytics group says, "Our management team wants us to be like Switzerland. We work only for the shareholders."

In fact, some senior executives push their analysts to play devil's advocate. This sets the right cultural tone and helps to refine the models. "All organizations seek to please the leader," explains Gary Loveman, of Caesars, "so it's critical to cultivate an environment that views ideas as separate from people and insists on rigorous evidence to distinguish among those ideas."

Loveman encourages his subordinates to put forth data and analysis, rather than opinions, and reveals his own faulty hypotheses, conclusions, and decisions. That way managers and quants alike understand that his sometimes "lame and ill-considered views," as he describes them, need as much objective, unbiased testing as anyone else's. For example, he often says that his greatest mistake as a new CEO was choosing not to fire property managers who didn't share his analytical orientation. He thought their experience would be enough. Loveman uses the example to show both that he's fallible and that he insists on being a consumer of analytics.

When It All Adds Up

Warren Buffett once said, "Beware of geeks . . . bearing formulas." But in today's data-driven world, you can't afford to do that. Instead you need to combine the science of analytics with the art of intuition. Be a manager who knows the geeks, understands their formulas, helps improve their analytic processes, effectively interprets and communicates the findings to others, and makes better decisions as a result.

Contrast the bank mentioned at the beginning of this article with Toronto-Dominion Bank. TD's CEO, Ed Clark, is quantitatively literate (with a PhD in economics), and he also insists that his managers understand the math behind any financial product the company depends on. As a result, TD knew to avoid the riskiest-structured products and get out of others before incurring major losses during the 2008–2009 financial crisis.

TD's emphasis on data and analytics affects other areas of the business as well. Compensation is closely tied to performance-management measures, for example. And TD's branches stay open longer than most other banks' because Tim Hockey, the former head of retail banking, insisted on systematically testing the effect of extended retail hours (with control groups) and found that they brought in more deposits. If anyone at a management meeting suggests a new direction, he or she is pressed for data and analysis to support it. TD is not perfect, Clark acknowledges, but "nobody ever accuses us of not running the numbers."

Your organization may not be as analytical as TD, and your CEO may not be like Ed Clark. But that doesn't mean you can't become a great consumer of analytics on your own—and set an example for the rest of your company.

———————

Thomas H. Davenport is the President's Distinguished Professor in Management and Information Technology at Babson College, a research fellow at the MIT Initiative on the Digital Economy, and a senior adviser at Deloitte Analytics. Author of over a dozen management books, his latest is *Only Humans Need Apply: Winners and Losers in the Age of Smart Machines.*

CHAPTER 2

A Simple Exercise to Help You Think Like a Data Scientist

by Thomas C. Redman

For 20 years, I've used a simple exercise to help those with an open mind (and a pencil, paper, and calculator) get started with data. One activity won't make you data savvy, but it will help you become data literate, open your eyes to the millions of small data opportunities, and enable you to work a bit more effectively with data scientists, analytics, and all things quantitative.

Adapted from "How to Start Thinking Like a Data Scientist" on hbr.org, November 29, 2013.

While the exercise is very much a how-to, each step also illustrates an important concept in analytics—from understanding variation to visualization.

First, start with something that interests, even bothers, you at work, like consistently late-starting meetings. Form it up as a question and write it down: "Meetings always seem to start late. Is that really true?"

Next, think through the data that can help answer your question and develop a plan for creating it. Write down all the relevant definitions and your protocol for collecting the data. For this particular example, you have to define when the meeting actually begins. Is it the time someone says, "OK, let's begin"? Or the time the real business of the meeting starts? Does kibitzing count?

Now collect the data. It is critical that you trust the data. And, as you go, you're almost certain to find gaps in data collection. You may find that even though a meeting has started, it starts anew when a more senior person joins in. Modify your definition and protocol as you go along.

Sooner than you think, you'll be ready to start drawing some pictures. Good pictures make it easier for you to both understand the data and communicate main points to others. There are plenty of good tools to help, but I like to draw my first picture by hand. My go-to plot is a time-series plot, where the horizontal axis has the date and time and the vertical axis has the variable of interest. Thus, a point on the graph in figure 2-1 is the date and time of a meeting versus the number of minutes late.

Now return to the question that you started with and develop summary statistics. Have you discovered an

FIGURE 2-1

How late are meetings?

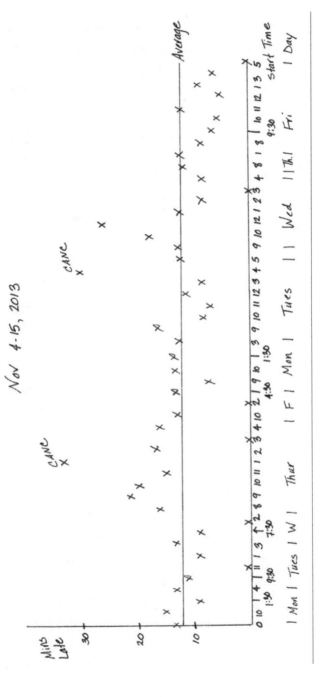

answer? In this case, "Over a two-week period, 10% of the meetings I attended started on time. And on average, they started 12 minutes late."

But don't stop there. Ask yourself, "So what?" In this case, "If those two weeks are typical, I waste an hour a day. And that costs the company x dollars a year."

Many analyses end because there is no "so what?" Certainly if 80% of meetings start within a few minutes of their scheduled start times, the answer to the original question is, "No, meetings start pretty much on time," and there is no need to go further.

But this case demands more, as some analyses do. Get a feel for variation. Understanding variation leads to a better feel for the overall problem, deeper insights, and novel ideas for improvement. Note on the graph that 8–20 minutes late is typical. A few meetings start right on time, others nearly a full 30 minutes late. It would be great if you could conclude, "I can get to meetings 10 minutes late, just in time for them to start," but the variation is too great.

Now ask, "What else does the data reveal?" It strikes me that six meetings began exactly on time, while every other meeting began at least seven minutes late. In this case, bringing meeting notes to bear reveals that all six on-time meetings were called by the vice president of finance. Evidently, she starts all her meetings on time.

So where do you go from here? Are there important next steps? This example illustrates a common dichotomy. On a personal level, results pass both the "interesting" and "important" test. Most of us would give almost anything to get back an hour a day. And you may not be able to make all meetings start on time, but if the VP can, you can certainly start the meetings you control promptly.

On the company level, results so far pass only the interesting test. You don't know whether your results are typical, nor whether others can be as hard-nosed as the VP when it comes to starting meetings. But a deeper look is surely in order: Are your results consistent with others' experiences in the company? Are some days worse than others? Which starts later: conference calls or face-to-face meetings? Is there a relationship between meeting start time and most senior attendee? Return to step one, pose the next group of questions, and repeat the process. Keep the focus narrow—two or three questions at most.

I hope you'll have fun with this exercise. Many find joy in teasing insights from data. But whether you experience that joy or not, don't take this exercise lightly. There are fewer and fewer places for the "data illiterate" and, in my humble opinion, no more excuses.

Thomas C. Redman, "the Data Doc," is President of Data Quality Solutions. He helps companies and people, including startups, multinationals, executives, and leaders at all levels, chart their courses to data-driven futures. He places special emphasis on quality, analytics, and organizational capabilities.

Gather the Right Information

CHAPTER 3

Do You Need All That Data?

by Ron Ashkenas

Organizations love data: numbers, reports, trend lines, graphs, spreadsheets—the more the better. And, as a result, many organizations have a substantial internal factory that churns out data on a regular basis, as well as external resources on call that produce data for onetime studies and questions. But what's the evidence (or dare I say "the data") that all this data leads to better business decisions? Is some amount of data collection unnecessary, and perhaps even damaging by creating complexity and confusion?

Let's look at a quick case study: For many years the CEO of a premier consumer products company insisted

Adapted from content posted on hbr.org, March 1, 2010 (product #H004FC).

on a monthly business review process that was highly data-intensive. At its core was a "book" that contained cost and sales data for every product sold by the company, broken down by business unit, channel, geography, and consumer segment. This book (available electronically but always printed by the executive team) was several inches thick. It was produced each month by many hundreds of finance, product management, and information technology people who spent thousands of hours collecting, assessing, analyzing, reconciling, and sorting the data.

Since this was the CEO's way of running the business, no one really questioned whether all of this activity was worth it, although many complained about the time required. When a new CEO came on the scene a couple of years ago, however, he decided that the business would do just fine with quarterly reviews and exception-only reporting. Suddenly the entire data-production industry of the company was reduced substantially—and the company didn't miss a beat.

Obviously, different CEOs have different needs for data. Some want their decisions to be based on as much hard data as possible; others want just enough to either reinforce or challenge their intuition; and still others may prefer a combination of hard, analytical data with anecdotal and qualitative input. In all cases, though, managers would do well to ask themselves four questions about their data process as a way of improving the return on what is often a substantial (but not always visible) investment:

1. **Are we asking the right questions?** Many companies collect the data that is available, rather than the information that is needed to help make decisions and run the business. So the starting point is to be clear about a limited number of key questions that you want the data to help you answer—and then focus the data collection around those rather than everything else that is possible.

2. **Does our data tell a story?** Most data comes in fragments. To be useful, these individual bits of information need to be put together into a coherent explanation of the business situation, which means integrating data into a "story." While enterprise data systems have been useful in driving consistent data definitions so that points can be added and compared, they don't automatically create the story. Instead, managers should consider in advance what data is needed to convey the story that they will be required to tell.

3. **Does our data help us look ahead rather than behind?** Most of the data that is collected in companies tells managers how they performed in a past period—but is less effective in predicting future performance. Therefore, it is important to ask what data, in what time frames, will help us get ahead of the curve instead of just reacting.

4. **Do we have a good mix of quantitative and qualitative data?** Neither quantitative nor qualitative data tells the whole story. For example, to make

good product and pricing decisions, we need to know not only what is being sold to whom, but also why some products are selling more than others.

Clearly, business data and its analysis are critical for organizations to succeed, which is underscored by the fact that companies like IBM are investing billions of dollars in acquisitions in the business intelligence and analytics space. But even the best automated tools won't be effective unless managers are clear about these four questions.

Ron Ashkenas is an Emeritus Partner with Schaffer Consulting, a frequent contributor to *Harvard Business Review*, and the author or coauthor of four books on organizational transformation. He has worked with hundreds of managers over the years to help them translate strategy into results and simplify the way things get done. He also is the coauthor (with Brook Manville) of *The Harvard Business Review Leader's Handbook* (Harvard Business Review Press; forthcoming in 2018). He can be reached at rashkenas@gmail.com.

CHAPTER 4

How to Ask Your Data Scientists for Data and Analytics

by Michael Li, Madina Kassengaliyeva, and Raymond Perkins

The intersection of big data and business is growing daily. Although enterprises have been studying analytics for decades, data science is a relatively new capability. And interacting in a new data-driven culture can be difficult, particularly for those who aren't data experts.

One particular challenge that many of these individuals face is how to request new data or analytics from data scientists. They don't know the right questions to ask, the correct terms to use, or the range of factors to consider to get the information they need. In the end, analysts are left uncertain about how to proceed, and managers are frustrated when the information they get isn't what they intended.

At The Data Incubator, we work with hundreds of companies looking to hire data scientists and data engineers or enroll their employees in our corporate training programs. We often field questions from our hiring and training clients about how to interact with their data experts. While it's impossible to give an exhaustive account, here are some important factors to think about when communicating with data scientists, particularly as you begin a data search.

What Question Should We Ask?

As you begin working with your data analysts, be clear about what you hope to achieve. Think about the business impact you want the data to have and the company's ability to act on that information. By hearing what you hope to gain from their assistance, the data scientist can collaborate with you to define the right set of questions to answer and better understand exactly what information to seek.

Even the subtlest ambiguity can have major implications. For example, advertising managers may ask analysts, "What is the most efficient way to use ads to increase sales?" Though this seems reasonable, it may not be the right question since the ultimate objective of most firms isn't to increase sales, but to maximize profit. Research from the Institute of Practitioners in Advertising shows that using ads to reduce price sensitivity is typically twice as profitable as trying to increase sales.[1] The value of the insight obtained will depend heavily on the question asked. Be as specific and actionable as possible.

What Data Do We Need?

As you define the right question and objectives for analysis, you and your data scientist should assess the availability of the data. Ask if someone has already collected the relevant data and performed analysis. The ever-growing breadth of public data often provides easily accessible answers to common questions. Cerner, a supplier of health care IT solutions, uses data sets from the U.S. Department of Health and Human Services to supplement their own data. iMedicare uses information from the Centers for Medicare and Medicaid Services to select policies. Consider whether public data could be used toward your problem as well. You can also work with other analysts in the organization to determine if the data has previously been examined for similar reasons by others internally.

Then, assess whether the available data is sufficient. Data may not contain all the relevant information needed to answer your questions. It may also be influenced by latent factors that can be difficult to recognize. Consider the vintage effect in private lending data: Even seemingly identical loans typically perform very differently based on the time of issuance, despite the fact they may have had identical data at that time. The effect comes from fluctuations in the underlying underwriting standards at issuance, information that is not typically represented in loan data.

You should also inquire if the data is unbiased, since sample size alone is not sufficient to guarantee its validity. Finally, ask if the data scientist has enough data to answer the question. By identifying what information is needed, you can help data scientists plan better analyses going forward.

How Do We Obtain the Data?

If more information is needed, data scientists must decide between using data compiled by the company through the normal course of business, such as through observational studies, and collecting new data through experiments. As part of your conversation with analysts, ask about the costs and benefits of these options. Observational studies may be easier and less expensive to arrange since they do not require direct interaction with subjects, for example, but they are typically far less reliable than experiments because they are only able to establish correlation, not causation.

Experiments allow substantially more control and provide more reliable information about causality, but they are often expensive and difficult to perform. Even seemingly harmless experiments may carry ethical or social implications with real financial consequences. Facebook, for example, faced public fury over its manipulation of its own newsfeed to test how emotions spread on social media. Though the experiments were completely legal, many users resented being unwitting participants in Facebook's tests. Managers must think beyond the data and consider the greater brand repercussions of data collection and work with data scientists to understand these consequences. (See the sidebar, "Understanding the Cost of Data.")

Before investing resources in new analysis, validate that the company can use the insights derived from it in a productive and meaningful way. This may entail integration with existing technology projects, providing new data to automated systems, and establishing new processes.

UNDERSTANDING THE COST OF DATA

Though effective data analysis has been shown to generate substantial financial gains, there can be many different costs and complexities associated with it. Obtaining good data may not only be difficult, but very expensive. For example, in the health care and pharmaceutical industry, data collection is often associated with medical experimentation and patient observations. These randomized control trials can easily cost millions. Data storage can cost millions annually as well. When interacting with data scientists, managers should ask about the specific risks and costs associated with obtaining and analyzing the data before moving forward with a project.

But not all costs associated with data collection are financial. Violations of user privacy can have enormous legal and reputational repercussions. Privacy is one of the most significant concerns regarding consumer data. Managers must consider and weigh the legal and ethical implications of their data collection and analysis methods. Even seemingly anonymized data can be used to identify individuals. Safely anonymized

(continued)

UNDERSTANDING THE COST OF DATA

(*continued*)

data can be de-anonymized when combined with other data sets. In a famous case, Carnegie Mellon University researchers were able to identify anonymized health care records of a former Massachusetts governor using only his ZIP code, birthday, and gender.[2] The Gartner Data Center predicted that through 2016, over 25% of firms using consumer data would incur reputation damage due to privacy violation issues.[3] Managers must ask data scientists about these risks when working with the company's potentially sensitive consumer data.

Is the Data Clean and Easy to Analyze?

In general, data comes in two forms: structured and unstructured. Structured data is structured, as its name implies, and easy to add to a database. Most analysts find it easier and faster to manipulate. Unstructured data is often free form and cannot be as easily stored in the types of relational databases most commonly used in enterprises. While unstructured data is estimated to make up 95% of the world's data, according to a report by professors Amir Gandomi and Murtaza Haider of Ryerson University, for many large companies, storing and manipulating unstructured data may require a significant investment of resources to extract necessary information.[4] Working with your data scientists, evaluate the additional costs of using unstructured data when defining your initial objectives.

Even if the data is structured it still may need to be cleaned or checked for incompleteness and inaccuracies. When possible, encourage analysts to use clean data first. Otherwise, they will have to waste valuable time and resources identifying and correcting inaccurate records. A 2014 survey conducted by Ascend2, a marketing research company, found that nearly 54% of respondents complained that a "lack of data quality/completeness" was their most prominent impediment. By searching for clean data, you can avoid significant problems and loss of time.

Is the Model Too Complicated?

Statistical techniques and open-source tools to analyze data abound, but simplicity is often the best choice. More complex and flexible tools expose themselves to overfitting and can take more time to develop (read more about overfitting in chapter 15, "Pitfalls of Data-Driven Decisions"). Work with your data scientists to identify the simpler techniques and tools and move to more complex models only if the simpler ones prove insufficient. It is important to observe the *KISS* rule: "Keep It Simple, Stupid!"

It may not be possible to avoid all of the expenses and issues related to data collection and analysis. But you can take steps to mitigate these costs and risks. By asking the right questions of your analysts, you can ensure proper collaboration and get the information you need to move forward confidently.

Michael Li is the founder and executive director of The Data Incubator, a big data company that trains and places data scientists. A data scientist himself, he has worked at Google, Foursquare, and Andreessen Horowitz. He is a regular contributor to VentureBeat, *The Next Web*, and *Harvard Business Review*. **Madina Kassengaliyeva** is a client services director with Think Big, a Teradata company. She helps clients realize high-impact business opportunities through effective implementation of big data and analytics solutions. Madina has managed accounts in the financial services and insurance industries and led successful strategy, solution development, and analytics engagements. **Raymond Perkins** is a researcher at Princeton University working at the intersection of statistics, data, and finance and is the executive director of the Princeton Quant Trading Conference. He has also conducted research at Hong Kong University of Science and Technology, the Mathematical Sciences Research Institute (MSRI), and Michigan State University.

NOTES

1. P. F. Mouncey, "Marketing in the Era of Accountability," *Journal of Direct, Data and Digital Marketing Practice* 9, no. 2 (December 2007): 225–228.

2. N. Anderson, "'Anonymized' Data Really Isn't—and Here's Why Not," Ars Technica, September 8, 2009, https://arstechnica.com/tech-policy/2009/09/your-secrets-live-online-in-databases-of-ruin/.

3. D. Laney, "Information Innovation Key Initiative Overview," Gartner Research, April 22, 2014, https://www.gartner.com/doc/2715317/information-innovation-key-initiative-overview.

4. A. Gandomi and M. Haider, "Beyond the Hype: Big Data Concepts, Methods, and Analytics," *International Journal of Information Management* 35, no. 2 (April 2015): 137–144.

CHAPTER 5

How to Design a Business Experiment

by Oliver Hauser and Michael Luca

The rise of experimental evaluations within organizations—or what economists refer to as field experiments—has the potential to transform organizational decision making, providing fresh insight into areas ranging from product design to human resources to public policy. Companies that invest in randomized evaluations can gain a game-changing advantage.

Yet while there has been a rapid growth in experiments, especially within tech companies, we've seen too

---

Adapted from "How to Design (and Analyze) a Business Experiment" on hbr.org, October 29, 2015 (product #H02FSL).

many run incorrectly. Even when they're set up properly, avoidable mistakes often happen during implementation. As a result, many organizations fail to receive the real benefits of the scientific method.

This chapter lays out seven steps to ensure that your experiment delivers the data and insight you need. These principles draw on the academic research on field experiments as well as our work with a variety of organizations ranging from Yelp to the UK government.

1. Identify a Narrow Question

It is tempting to run an experiment around a question such as "Is advertising worth the cost?" or "Should we reduce (or increase) our annual bonuses?" Indeed, beginning with a question that is central to your broader goals is a good start. But it's misguided to think that a single experiment will do the trick. The reason is simple: Multiple factors go into answering these types of big questions.

Take the issue of whether advertising is worth the cost. What form of advertising are we talking about, and for which products, in which media, over which time periods? Your question should be testable, which means it must be narrow and clearly defined. A better question might be, "How much does advertising our brand name on Google AdWords increase monthly sales?" This is an empirical question that an experiment can answer—and that feeds into the question you ultimately hope to resolve. In fact, through just such an experiment, researchers at eBay discovered that a long-standing brand-advertising strategy on Google had no effect on the rate at which paying customers visited eBay.

2. Use a Big Hammer

Companies experiment when they don't know what will work best. Faced with this uncertainty, it may sound appealing to start small in order to avoid disrupting things. But your goal should be to see whether some version of your intervention—your new change—will make a difference to your customers. This requires a large-enough intervention.

For example, suppose a grocery store is considering adding labels to items to show consumers that it sources mainly from local farms. How big should the labels be and where should they be attached? We would suggest starting with large labels on the front of the packages, because if the labels were small or on the backs of the packages, and there were no effect (a common outcome for subtle interventions), the store managers would be left to wonder whether consumers simply didn't notice the tags (the treatment wasn't large enough) or truly didn't care (there was no treatment effect). By starting with a big hammer, the store would learn whether customers care about local sourcing. If there's no effect from large labels on the package fronts, then the store should give up on the idea. If there *is* an effect, the experimenters can later refine the labels to the desired characteristics.

3. Perform a Data Audit

Once you know what your intervention is, you need to choose what data to look at. Make a list of all the internal data related to the outcome you would like to influence and when you will need to do the measurements.

Include data both about things you hope will change and things you hope *won't* change as a result of the intervention, because you'll need to be alert for unintended consequences. Think, too, about sources of external data that might add perspective.

Say you're launching a new cosmetics product and you want to know which type of packaging leads to the highest customer loyalty and satisfaction. You decide to run a randomized controlled trial across geographical areas. In addition to measuring recurring orders and customer service feedback (internal data), you can track user reviews on Amazon and look for differences among customers in different states (external data).

4. Select a Study Population

Choose a subgroup among your customers that matches the customer profile you are hoping to understand. It might be tempting to look for the easiest avenue to get a subgroup, such as online users, but beware: If your subgroup is not a good representation of your target customers, the findings of your experiment may not be applicable. For example, younger online customers who shop exclusively on your e-commerce platform may behave very differently than older in-store customers. You could use the former to generalize to your online platform strategy, but you may be misguided if you try to draw inferences from that group for your physical stores.

5. Randomize

Randomly assign some people to a treatment group and others to a control group. The treatment group receives the change you want to test, while the control group receives what you previously had on offer—and make sure there are no differences other than what you are testing. The first rule of randomization is to not let participants decide which group they are in, or the results will be meaningless. The second is to make sure there really are no differences between treatment and control.

It's not always easy to follow the second rule. For example, we've seen companies experiment by offering a different coupon on Sunday than on Monday. The problem is that Sunday shoppers may be systematically different from Monday shoppers, even if you control for the volume of shoppers on each day.

6. Commit to a Plan, and Stick to It

Before you run an experiment, lay out your plans in detail. How many observations will you collect? How long will you let the experiment run? What variables will be collected and analyzed? Record these details. This can be as simple as creating a Google spreadsheet or as official as using a public trial registry. Not only will this level of transparency make sure that everyone is on the same page, it will also help you avoid well-known pitfalls in the implementation of experiments.

Once your experiment is running, leave it alone! If you get a result you expected, great; if not, that's fine too. The one thing that's not OK: running your experiment until your results look as though they fit your hypothesis, rather than until the study has run its planned course. This type of practice has led to a "replication crisis" in psychology research; it can seriously bias your results and reduce the insight you receive. Stick to the plan, to the extent possible.

7. Let the Data Speak

To give a complete picture of your results, report multiple outcomes. Sure, some might be unchanged, unimpressive, or downright inexplicable. But better to be transparent about them than to ignore them. Once you've surveyed the main results, ask yourself whether you've really discovered the underlying mechanism behind your results—the factor that is driving them. If you're not sure, refine your experiment and run another trial to learn more.

Experiments are already a central part of the social sciences; they are quickly becoming central to organizations as well. If your experiments are well designed, they will tell you something valuable. The most successful will puncture your assumptions, change your practices, and put you ahead of competitors. Experimentation is a long-term, richly informative process, with each trial forming the starting point for the next.

Oliver Hauser is a research fellow at Harvard Business School and Harvard Kennedy School. He conducts research and runs experiments with organizations and governments around the world. **Michael Luca** is the Lee J. Styslinger III Associate Professor of Business Administration at Harvard Business School and works with a variety of organizations to design experiments.

CHAPTER 6

Know the Difference Between Your Data and Your Metrics

by Jeff Bladt and Bob Filbin

How many views make a YouTube video a success? How about 1.5 million? That's how many views a video posted in 2011 by our organization, DoSomething.org, received. It featured some well-known YouTube celebrities, who asked young people to donate their used sports equipment to youth in need. It was twice as popular as any video DoSomething.org had posted to date. Success! Then came the data report: only eight viewers had signed up to donate equipment, and no one actually donated.

Adapted from content posted on hbr.org, March 4, 2013.

Zero donations from 1.5 million views. Suddenly, it was clear that for DoSomething.org, views did not equal success. In terms of donations, the video was a complete failure.

What happened? We were concerned with the wrong metric. A metric contains a single type of data—video views or equipment donations. A successful organization can only measure so many things well and what it measures ties to its definition of success. For DoSomething.org, that's social change. In the case above, success meant donations, not video views. As we learned, there is a difference between numbers and numbers that matter. This is what separates data from metrics.

You Can't Pick Your Data, but You Must Pick Your Metrics

Take baseball. Every team has the same definition of success—winning the World Series. This requires one main asset: good players. But what makes a player good? In baseball, teams used to answer this question with a handful of simple metrics like batting average and runs batted in (RBIs). Then came the statisticians (remember *Moneyball*?). New metrics provided teams with the ability to slice their data in new ways, find better ways of defining good players, and thus win more games.

Keep in mind that all metrics are proxies for what ultimately matters (in the case of baseball, a combination of championships and profitability), but some are better than others. The data of the game has never changed—there are still RBIs and batting averages. What has changed is how we look at the data. And those teams that slice the data in smarter ways are able to find good players who have been traditionally undervalued.

Organizations Become Their Metrics

Metrics are what you measure. And what you measure is what you manage to. In baseball, a critical question is, how effective is a player when he steps up to the plate? One measure is hits. A better measure turns out to be the sabermetric "OPS"—a combination of on-base percentage (which includes hits and walks) and total bases (slugging). Teams that look only at batting average suffer. Players on these teams walk less, with no offsetting gains in hits. In short, players play to the metrics their management values, even at the cost of the team.

The same happens in workplaces. Measure YouTube views? Your employees will strive for more and more views. Measure downloads of a product? You'll get more of that. But if your actual goal is to boost sales or acquire members, better measures might be return-on-investment (ROI), on-site conversion, or retention. Do people who download the product keep using it or share it with others? If not, all the downloads in the world won't help your business. (See the sidebar, "Picking Statistics," to learn how to choose metrics that that align with a specific performance objective.)

In the business world, we talk about the difference between vanity metrics and meaningful metrics. Vanity metrics are like dandelions—they might look pretty, but to most of us, they're weeds, using up resources and doing nothing for your property value. Vanity metrics for your organization might include website visitors per month, Twitter followers, Facebook fans, and media impressions. Here's the thing: If these numbers go up, they might drive up sales of your product. But can you prove it? If yes, great. Measure away. But if you can't, they aren't valuable.

PICKING STATISTICS

by Michael Mauboussin

The following is a process for choosing metrics that allow you to understand, track, and manage the cause-and-effect relationships that determine your company's performance. I will illustrate the process in a simplified way using a retail bank that is based on an analysis of 115 banks by Venky Nagar of the University of Michigan and Madhav Rajan of Stanford. Leave aside, for the moment, which metrics you currently use or which ones Wall Street analysts or bankers say you should. Start with a blank slate and work through these four steps in sequence.

1. Define Your Governing Objective

A clear objective is essential to business success because it guides the allocation of capital. Creating economic value is a logical governing objective for a company that operates in a free market system. Companies may choose a different objective, such as maximizing the firm's longevity. We will assume that the retail bank seeks to create economic value.

2. Develop a Theory of Cause and Effect to Assess Presumed Drivers of the Objective

The three commonly cited financial drivers of value creation are sales, costs, and investments. More-specific financial drivers vary among companies and can include earnings growth, cash flow growth, and return on invested capital.

Naturally, financial metrics can't capture all value-creating activities. You also need to assess nonfinancial measures such as customer loyalty, customer satisfaction, and product quality, and determine if they can be directly linked to the financial measures that ultimately deliver value. As we've discussed, the link between value creation and financial and nonfinancial measures like these is variable and must be evaluated on a case-by-case basis.

In our example, the bank starts with the theory that customer satisfaction drives the use of bank services and that usage is the main driver of value. This theory links a nonfinancial and a financial driver. The bank then measures the correlations statistically to see if the theory is correct and determines that satisfied customers indeed use more services, allowing the bank to

(continued)

PICKING STATISTICS

(continued)

generate cash earnings growth and attractive returns on assets, both indicators of value creation. Having determined that customer satisfaction is persistently and predictively linked to returns on assets, the bank must now figure out which employee activities drive satisfaction.

3. Identify the Specific Activities That Employees Can Do to Help Achieve the Governing Objective

The goal is to make the link between your objective and the measures that employees can control through the application of skill. The relationship between these activities and the objective must also be persistent and predictive.

In the previous step, the bank determined that customer satisfaction drives value (it is predictive). The bank now has to find reliable drivers of customer satisfaction. Statistical analysis shows that the rates consumers receive on their loans, the speed of loan processing, and low teller turnover all affect customer satisfaction. Because these are within the control of employees and management, they are persistent. The bank can use this information to, for example, make sure that its process for reviewing and approving loans is quick and efficient.

4. Evaluate Your Statistics

Finally, you must regularly reevaluate the measures you are using to link employee activities with the governing objective. The drivers of value change over time, and so must your statistics. For example, the demographics of the retail bank's customer base are changing, so the bank needs to review the drivers of customer satisfaction. As the customer base becomes younger and more digitally savvy, teller turnover becomes less relevant and the bank's online interface and customer service become more so. Companies have access to a growing torrent of statistics that could improve their performance, but executives still cling to old-fashioned and often flawed methods for choosing metrics. In the past, companies could get away with going on gut and ignoring the right statistics because that's what everyone else was doing. Today, using them is necessary to compete. More to the point, identifying and exploiting them before rivals do will be the key to seizing advantage.

Excerpted from "The True Measures of Success" in *Harvard Business Review,* October 2012 (product #R1210B).

Michael Mauboussin is an investment strategist and an adjunct professor at Columbia Business School. His latest book is *The Success Equation* (Harvard Business Review Press, 2012).

Metrics Are Only Valuable if You Can Manage to Them

Good metrics have three key attributes: Their data is consistent, cheap, and quick to collect. A simple rule of thumb: If you can't measure results within a week for free (and if you can't replicate the process), then you're prioritizing the wrong ones. There are exceptions, but they are rare. In baseball, the metrics an organization uses to measure a successful plate appearance will affect player strategy in the short term (do they draw more walks, prioritize home runs, etc.?) and personnel strategy in the mid- and long terms. The data to make these decisions is readily available and continuously updated.

Organizations can't control their data, but they do control what they care about. If our metric on the YouTube video had been views, we would have called it a huge success. In fact, we wrote it off as a massive failure. Does that mean no more videos? Not necessarily, but for now, we'll be spending our resources elsewhere, collecting data on metrics that matter.

Jeff Bladt is chief data officer at DoSomething.org, America's largest organization for young people and social change. **Bob Filbin** is chief data scientist at Crisis Text Line, the first large-scale 24/7 national crisis line for teens on the medium they use most: texting.

CHAPTER 7

The Fundamentals of A/B Testing

by Amy Gallo

As we learned in chapter 5, running an experiment is a straightforward way to collect new data about a specific question or problem. One of the most common methods of experimentation, particularly in online settings, is A/B testing.

To better understand what A/B testing is, where it originated, and how to use it, I spoke with Kaiser Fung, who founded the applied analytics program at Columbia University and is author of *Junk Charts*, a blog devoted to the critical examination of data and graphics in the mass media. His latest book is *Numbersense: How to Use Big Data to Your Advantage.*

Adapted from "A Refresher on A/B Testing" on hbr.org, June 28, 2017 (product #H03R3D).

What Is A/B Testing?

A/B testing is a way to compare two versions of something to figure out which performs better. While it's most often associated with websites and apps, Fung says the method is almost 100 years old.

In the 1920s, statistician and biologist Ronald Fisher discovered the most important principles behind A/B testing and randomized controlled experiments in general. "He wasn't the first to run an experiment like this, but he was the first to figure out the basic principles and mathematics and make them a science," Fung says.

Fisher ran agricultural experiments, asking questions such as, "What happens if I put more fertilizer on this land?" The principles persisted, and in the early 1950s scientists started running clinical trials in medicine. In the 1960s and 1970s, the concept was adapted by marketers to evaluate direct-response campaigns (for example, "Would a postcard or a letter sent to target customers result in more sales?").

A/B testing in its current form came into existence in the 1990s. Fung says that throughout the past century, the math behind the tests hasn't changed: "It's the same core concepts, but now you're doing it online, in a real-time environment, and on a different scale in terms of number of participants and number of experiments."

How Does A/B Testing Work?

You start an A/B test by deciding what it is you want to test. Fung gives a simple example: the size of the "Subscribe" button on your website. Then you need to know how you want to evaluate its performance. In this case, let's say your metric is the number of visitors who click on the button. To run the test, you show two sets of users (assigned at random when they visit the site) the different versions (where the only thing different is the size of the button) and determine which influenced your success metric the most—in this case, which button size caused more visitors to click.

There are a lot of things that influence whether someone clicks. For example, it may be that those using a mobile device are more likely to click a button of a certain size, while those on desktop are drawn to a different size. This is where randomization is critical. By randomizing which users are in which group, you minimize the chances that other factors, like mobile versus desktop, will drive your results on average.

"The A/B test can be considered the most basic kind of randomized controlled experiment," Fung says. "In its simplest form, there are two treatments and one acts as the control for the other." As with all randomized controlled experiments, you must estimate the sample size you need to achieve a statistical significance, which will help you make sure the result you're seeing "isn't just because of background noise," Fung says.

Sometimes you know that certain variables, usually those that are not easily manipulated, have a strong effect on the success metric. For example, maybe mobile users of your website tend to click less in general, compared with desktop users. Randomization may result in set A containing slightly more mobile users than set B, which may cause set A to have a lower click rate regardless of the button size they're seeing. To level the playing field, the test analyst should first divide the users by mobile and desktop and then randomly assign them to each version. This is called *blocking*.

The size of the "Subscribe" button is a very basic example, Fung says. In actuality, you might not be testing just size but also color, text, typeface, and font size. Lots of managers run sequential tests—testing size first (large versus small), then color (blue versus red), then typeface (Times versus Arial), and so on—because they believe they shouldn't vary two or more factors at the same time. But according to Fung, that view has been debunked by statisticians. Sequential tests are in fact suboptimal, because you're not measuring what happens when factors interact. For example, it may be that users prefer blue on average but prefer red when it's combined with an Arial font. This kind of result is regularly missed in sequential A/B testing because the typeface test is run on blue buttons that have "won" the previous test.

Instead, Fung says, you should run more-complex tests. This can be hard for some managers, since the appeal of A/B tests is how straightforward and simple they are to run (and many people designing these experiments, Fung points out, don't have a statistics background). "With A/B testing, we tend to want to run a large number of simultaneous, independent tests," he says, in large part because the mind reels at the number of possible combinations that can be tested. But using mathematics, you can "smartly pick and run only certain subsets of those treatments; then you can infer the rest from the data." This is called *multivariate* testing in the A/B testing world, and it means you often end up doing an A/B/C test or even an A/B/C/D test. In the colors and size example, it might include showing different groups a large red button, a small red button, a large blue button, and a small blue button. If you wanted to test fonts too, you would need even more test groups.

How Do You Interpret the Results of an A/B Test?

Chances are that your company will use software that handles the calculations, and it may even employ a statistician who can interpret those results for you. But it's helpful to have a basic understanding of how to make sense of the output and decide whether to move forward with the test variation (the new button, in the example Fung describes).

Fung says that most software programs report two conversion rates for A/B testing: one for users who saw the control version, and the other for users who saw the test version. "The conversion rate may measure clicks or other actions taken by users," he says. The report might look like this: "Control: 15% (+/− 2.1%); Variation 18% (+/− 2.3%)." This means that 18% of your users clicked through on the new variation (perhaps the larger blue button) with a margin of error of 2.3%. You might be tempted to interpret this as the actual conversion rate falling between 15.7% and 20.3%, but that wouldn't be technically correct. "The real interpretation is that if you ran your A/B test multiple times, 95% of the ranges will capture the true conversion rate—in other words, the conversion rate falls outside the margin of error 5% of the time (or whatever level of statistical significance you've set)," Fung explains.

This can be a difficult concept to wrap your head around. But what's important to know is that the 18% conversion rate isn't a guarantee. This is where your judgment comes in. An 18% conversation rate is certainly better than a 15% one, even allowing for the margin of error (12.9% to 17.1% versus 15.7% to 20.3%). You might hear people talk about this as a "3% lift" (*lift* is the percentage difference in conversion rate between your control version and a successful test treatment). In this case, it's most likely a good decision to switch to your new version, but that will depend on the costs of implementing it. If they're low, you might try out the switch and see what happens in actuality (versus in tests). One of the big advantages to testing in the online world is that you can usually revert back to your original pretty easily.

How Do Companies Use A/B Testing?

Fung says that the popularity of the methodology has risen as companies have realized that the online environment is well suited to help managers, especially marketers, answer questions like, "What is most likely to make people click? Or buy our product? Or register with our site?" A/B testing is now used to evaluate everything from website design to online offers to headlines to product descriptions. (See the sidebar "A/B Testing in

Action" to see an example from the creative marketplace Shutterstock.)

Most of these experiments run without the subjects even knowing. As users, Fung says, "we're part of these tests all the time and don't know it."

And it's not just websites. You can test marketing emails or ads as well. For example, you might send two versions of an email to your customer list (randomizing the list first, of course) and figure out which one generates more sales. Then you can just send out the winning version next time. Or you might test two versions of ad copy and see which one converts visitors more often. Then you know to spend more getting the most successful one out there.

A/B TESTING IN ACTION

by Wyatt Jenkins

At Shutterstock, we test everything: copy and link colors, relevance algorithms that rank our search results, language-detection functions, usability in downloading, pricing, video-playback design, and anything else you can see on our site (plus a lot you can't).

Shutterstock is the world's largest creative marketplace, serving photography, illustrations, and video to more than 750,000 customers. And those customers

(continued)

A/B TESTING IN ACTION

(*continued*)

have heavy image needs; we serve over three downloads per second. That's a ton of data.

This means that we know more about our customers, statistically, than anyone else in our market. It also means that we can run more experiments with statistical significance faster than businesses with less user data. It's one of our most important competitive advantages.

Search results are among the highest-trafficked pages on our site. A few years back, we started experimenting with a mosaic-display search-results page in our Labs area—an experimentation platform we use to try things quickly and get user feedback. In qualitative testing, customers really liked the design of the mosaic search grid, so we A/B tested it within the core Shutterstock experience.

Here are some of the details of the experiment, and what we learned:

- *Image sizes:* We tested different image sizes to get just the right number of pixels on the screen.

- *New customers:* We watched to see if new customers to our site would increase conversion. New customers act differently than existing ones, so you need to account for that. Sometimes existing customers suffer from change aversion.

- *Viewport size:* We tracked the viewport size (the size of the screen customers used) to understand how they were viewing the page.

- *Watermarks:* We tested including an image watermark versus no watermark. Was including the watermark distracting?

- *Hover:* We experimented with the behavior of a hover feature when a user paused on a particular image.

Before the test, we were convinced that removing the watermark on our images would increase conversion because there would be less visual clutter on the page. But in testing we learned that removing the watermark created the opposite effect, disproving our gut instinct.

We ran enough tests to find two different designs that increased conversion, so we iterated on those designs and re-tested them before deciding on one. And we continue to test this search grid and make improvements for our customers on a regular basis.

Adapted from "A/B Testing and the Benefits of an Experimentation Culture" posted on hbr.org, February 5, 2014 (product #HOONTO).

Wyatt Jenkins is a product executive with a focus on marketplaces, personalization, optimization, and international growth. He has acted as SVP of Product at Hired.com and Optimizely, and was VP of Product at Shutterstock for five years. Wyatt was an early partner in Beatport from 2003 to 2009, and he served on the board until 2013.

What Mistakes Do People Make When Doing A/B Tests?

Fung identified three common mistakes he sees companies make when performing A/B tests.

First, too many managers don't let the tests run their course. Because most of the software for running these tests lets you watch results in real time, managers want to make decisions too quickly. This mistake, Fung says, "evolves out of impatience," and many software vendors have played into this overeagerness by offering a type of A/B testing called *real-time optimization,* in which you can use algorithms to make adjustments as results come in. The problem is that, because of randomization, it's possible that if you let the test run to its natural end, you might get a different result.

The second mistake is looking at too many metrics. "I cringe every time I see software that tries to please everyone by giving you a panel of hundreds of metrics," he says. The problem is that if you're looking at such a large number of metrics at the same time, you're at risk of making what statisticians call *spurious correlations* (a topic discussed in more detail in chapter 10). In proper test design, "you should decide on the metrics you're going to look at before you execute an experiment and select a few. The more you're measuring, the more likely that you're going to see random fluctuations." With too many metrics, instead of asking yourself, "What's happening with this variable?" you're asking, "What interesting (and potentially insignificant) changes am I seeing?"

Lastly, Fung says, few companies do enough retesting. "We tend to test it once and then we believe it. But even with a statistically significant result, there's a quite large probability of false positive error. Unless you retest once in a while, you don't rule out the possibility of being wrong." False positives can occur for several reasons. For example, even though there may be little chance that any given A/B result is driven by random chance, if you do lots of A/B tests, the chances that at least one of your results is wrong grows rapidly.

This can be particularly difficult to do because it is likely that managers would end up with contradictory results, and no one wants to discover that they've undermined previous findings, especially in the online world, where managers want to make changes—and capture value—quickly. But this focus on value can be misguided. Fung says, "People are not very vigilant about the practical value of the findings. They want to believe that every little amount of improvement is valuable even when the test results are not fully reliable. In fact, the smaller the improvement, the less reliable the results."

It's clear that A/B testing is not a panacea for all your data-testing needs. There are more complex kinds of experiments that are more efficient and will give you more reliable data, Fung says. But A/B testing is a great way to gain quick information about a specific question you have, particularly in an online setting. And, as Fung says, "the good news about the A/B testing world is that everything happens so quickly, so if you run it and it doesn't work, you can try something else. You can always flip back to the old tactic."

Amy Gallo is a contributing editor at *Harvard Business Review* and the author of the *HBR Guide to Dealing with Conflict*. Follow her on Twitter @amyegallo.

CHAPTER 8

Can Your Data Be Trusted?

by Thomas C. Redman

You've just learned of some new data that, when combined with existing data, could offer potentially game-changing insights. But there isn't a clear indication whether this new information can be trusted. How should you proceed?

There is, of course, no simple answer. While many managers are skeptical of new data and others embrace it wholeheartedly, the more thoughtful managers take a nuanced approach. They know that some data (maybe even most of it) is bad and can't be used, and some is good and should be trusted implicitly. But they also realize that some data is flawed but usable with caution.

Adapted from content posted on hbr.org, October 29, 2015 (product #H02G61).

They find this data intriguing and are eager to push the data to its limits, as they know game-changing insights may reside there.

Fortunately, you can work with your data scientists to assess whether the data you're considering is safe to use and just how far you can go with flawed data. Indeed, following some basic steps can help you proceed with greater confidence—or caution—as the quality of the data dictates.

Evaluate Where It Came From

You can trust data when it is created in accordance with a first-rate data quality program. They feature clear accountabilities for managers to create data correctly, input controls, and find and eliminate the root causes of error. You won't have to opine whether the data is good—data quality statistics will tell you. You'll find an expert who will be happy to explain what you may expect and answer your questions. If the data quality stats look good and the conversation goes well, trust the data. This is the "gold standard" against which the other steps should be calibrated.

Assess Data Quality Independently

Much, perhaps most, data will not meet the gold standard, so adopt a cautious attitude by doing your own assessment of data quality. Make sure you know where the data was created and how it is defined, not just how your data scientist accessed it. It is easy to be misled by a casual, "We took it from our cloud-based data warehouse, which employs the latest technology," and completely miss the fact that the data was created in a dubious public forum. Figure out which organization created the data. Then dig deeper: What do colleagues advise about this organization and data? Does it have a good or poor reputation for quality? What do others say on social media? Do some research both inside and outside your company.

At the same time, develop your own data quality statistics, using what I call the "Friday afternoon measurement," tailor-made for this situation. Briefly, you, the data scientist providing the analysis, or both of you, should lay out 10 or 15 important data elements for 100 data records on a spreadsheet. If the new data involves customer purchases, such data elements may include "customer name," "purchased item," and "price." Then work record by record, taking a hard look at each data element. The obvious errors will jump out at you— customer names will be misspelled, the purchased item will be a product you don't sell, or the price may be missing. Mark these obvious errors with a red pen or highlight them in a bright color. Then count the number of records with no errors. (See figure 8-1 for an example.) In many cases you'll see a lot of red—don't trust this data! If you see only a little red, say, less than 5% of records with an obvious error, you can use this data with caution.

Look, too, at patterns of the errors. If, for instance, there are 25 total errors, 24 of which occur in the price, eliminate that data element going forward. But if the rest of the data looks pretty good, use it with caution.

FIGURE 8-1

Example: Friday afternoon measurement spreadsheet

Record	Attribute 1 Name	Attribute 2 Size	Attribute 3 Amount	Attribute 15	Perfect record?
1	Jane Doe	Null	$472.13		No
2	John Smith	Medium	$126.93		Yes
3	Stuart Madnick	XXXL	Null		No
4	Thoams Jones				No
100	James Olsen	24 Lockwood Road	$76.24		No

Number of
perfect records
= 67

Source: Thomas C. Redman, "Assess Whether You Have a Data Quality Problem" on hbr.org, July 28, 2016 (product #H030SQ).

Clean the Data

I think of data cleaning in three levels: rinse, wash, and scrub. "Rinse" replaces obvious errors with "missing value" or corrects them if doing so is very easy; "scrub" involves deep study, even making corrections one at a time, by hand, if necessary; and "wash" occupies a middle ground.

Even if time is short, scrub a small random sample (say, 1,000 records), making them as pristine as you possibly can. Your goal is to arrive at a sample of data you know you can trust. Employ all possible means of scrubbing and be ruthless! Eliminate erroneous data records and data elements that you cannot correct, and mark data as "uncertain" when applicable.

When you are done, take a hard look. When the scrubbing has gone really well (and you'll know if it has), you've created a data set that rates high on the trustworthy scale. It's OK to move forward using this data.

Sometimes the scrubbing is less satisfying. If you've done the best you can, but still feel uncertain, put this data in the "use with caution" category. If the scrubbing goes poorly—for example, too many prices just look wrong and you can't make corrections—you must rate this data, and all like it, as untrustworthy. The sample strongly suggests none of the data should be used to inform your decision.

After the initial scrub, move on to the second cleaning exercise: washing the remaining data that was not in the scrubbing sample. This step should be performed by a truly competent data scientist. Since scrubbing can be a time-consuming, manual process, the wash allows you to make corrections using more automatic processes. For example, one wash technique involves "imputing" missing values using statistical means. Or your data scientist may have discovered algorithms during scrubbing. If the washing goes well, put this data into the "use with caution" category.

The flow chart in figure 8-2 will help you see this process in action. Once you've identified a set of data that you can trust or use with caution, move on to the next step of integration.

Ensure High-Quality Data Integration

Align the data you can trust—or the data that you're moving forward with cautiously—with your existing data. There is a lot of technical work here, so probe your data scientist to ensure three things are done well:

- **Identification:** Verify that the Courtney Smith in one data set is the same Courtney Smith in others.

- **Alignment of units of measure and data definitions:** Make sure Courtney's purchases and prices paid, expressed in "pallets" and "dollars" in one set, are aligned with "units" and "euros" in another.

- **De-duplication:** Check that the Courtney Smith record does not appear multiple times in different ways (say as C. Smith or Courtney E. Smith).

At this point in the process, you're ready to perform whatever analytics (from simple summaries to more complex analyses) you need to guide your decision. Pay

FIGURE 8-2

Should you trust your data?

A simple process to help you decide

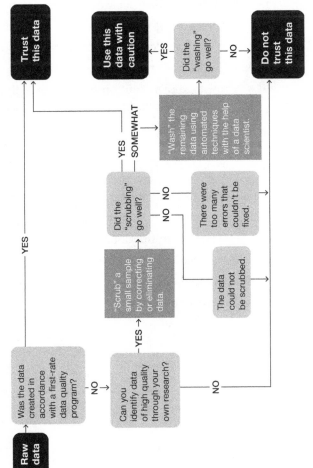

particular attention when you get different results based on "use with caution" and "trusted" data. Both great insights and great traps lie here. When a result looks intriguing, isolate the data and repeat the steps above, making more detailed measurements, scrubbing the data, and improving wash routines. As you do so, develop a feel for how deeply you should trust this data.

Data doesn't have to be perfect to yield new insights, but you must exercise caution by understanding where the flaws lie, working around errors, cleaning them up, and backing off when the data simply isn't good enough.

Thomas C. Redman, "the Data Doc," is President of Data Quality Solutions. He helps companies and people, including startups, multinationals, executives, and leaders at all levels, chart their courses to data-driven futures. He places special emphasis on quality, analytics, and organizational capabilities.

SECTION THREE

Analyze the Data

CHAPTER 9

A Predictive Analytics Primer

by Thomas H. Davenport

No one has the ability to capture and analyze data from the future. However, there is a way to predict the future using data from the past. It's called predictive analytics, and organizations do it every day.

Has your company, for example, developed a customer lifetime value (CLTV) measure? That's using predictive analytics to determine how much a customer will buy from the company over time. Do you have a "next best offer" or product recommendation capability? That's an analytical prediction of the product or service that your customer is most likely to buy next. Have you made a

Adapted from content posted on hbr.org, September 2, 2014 (product #H00YO1).

forecast of next quarter's sales? Used digital marketing models to determine what ad to place on what publisher's site? All of these are forms of predictive analytics.

Predictive analytics are gaining in popularity, but what do you really need to know in order to interpret results and make better decisions? By understanding a few basics, you will feel more comfortable working with and communicating with others in your organization about the results and recommendations from predictive analytics. The quantitative analysis isn't magic—but it is normally done with a lot of past data, a little statistical wizardry, and some important assumptions.

The Data

Lack of good data is the most common barrier to organizations seeking to employ predictive analytics. To make predictions about what customers will buy in the future, for example, you need to have good data on what they are buying (which may require a loyalty program, or at least a lot of analysis of their credit cards), what they have bought in the past, the attributes of those products (attribute-based predictions are often more accurate than the "people who buy this also buy this" type of model), and perhaps some demographic attributes of the customer (age, gender, residential location, socioeconomic status, etc.). If you have multiple channels or customer touchpoints, you need to make sure that they capture data on customer purchases in the same way your previous channels did.

All in all, it's a fairly tough job to create a single customer data warehouse with unique customer IDs on everyone, and all past purchases customers have made through all channels. If you've already done that, you've got an incredible asset for predictive customer analytics.

The Statistics

Regression analysis in its various forms is the primary tool that organizations use for predictive analytics. It works like this, in general: An analyst hypothesizes that a set of independent variables (say, gender, income, visits to a website) are statistically correlated with the purchase of a product for a sample of customers. The analyst performs a regression analysis to see just how correlated each variable is; this usually requires some iteration to find the right combination of variables and the best model. Let's say that the analyst succeeds and finds that each variable in the model is important in explaining the product purchase, and together the variables explain a lot of variation in the product's sales. Using that regression equation, the analyst can then use the regression coefficients—the degree to which each variable affects the purchase behavior—to create a score predicting the likelihood of the purchase.

Voilà! You have created a predictive model for other customers who weren't in the sample. All you have to do is compute their score and offer them the product if their score exceeds a certain level. It's quite likely that the high-scoring customers will want to buy the product—assuming the analyst did the statistical work well and that the data was of good quality. (For more on regression analysis, read on to the next chapter.)

The Assumptions

Another key factor in any predictive model is the assumptions that underlie it. Every model has them, and it's important to know what they are and monitor whether they are still true. The big assumption in predictive analytics is that the future will continue to be like the past. As Charles Duhigg describes in his book *The Power of Habit*, people establish strong patterns of behavior that they usually keep up over time. Sometimes, however, they change those behaviors, and the models that were used to predict them may no longer be valid.

What makes assumptions invalid? The most common reason is time. If your model was created several years ago, it may no longer accurately predict current behavior. The greater the elapsed time, the more likely it is that customer behavior has changed. Some Netflix predictive models, for example, that were created on early internet users had to be retired because later internet users were substantially different. The pioneers were more technically focused and relatively young; later users were essentially everyone.

Another reason a predictive model's assumptions may no longer be valid is if the analyst didn't include a key variable in the model, and that variable has changed substantially over time. The great—and scary—example here is the financial crisis of 2008–2009, caused largely by invalid models predicting how likely mortgage customers were to repay their loans. The models didn't include the possibility that housing prices might stop rising, and that they even might fall. When they did start falling, it turned out that the models were poor predictors of mortgage repayment. In essence, the belief that housing prices would always rise was a hidden assumption in the models.

Since faulty or obsolete assumptions can clearly bring down whole banks and even (nearly!) whole economies, it's pretty important that they be carefully examined. Managers should always ask analysts what the key assumptions are, and what would have to happen for them to no longer be valid. And both managers and analysts should continually monitor the world to see if key factors involved in assumptions have changed over time.

With these fundamentals in mind, here are a few good questions to ask your analysts:

- Can you tell me something about the source of the data you used in your analysis?

- Are you sure the sample data is representative of the population?

- Are there any outliers in your data distribution? How did they affect the results?

- What assumptions are behind your analysis?

- Are there any conditions that would make your assumptions invalid?

Even with those cautions, it's still pretty amazing that we can use analytics to predict the future. All we have to do is gather the right data, do the right type of statistical model, and be careful of our assumptions. Analytical predictions may be harder to generate than those by the late-night television soothsayer Carnac the Magnificent, but they are usually considerably more accurate.

———————

Thomas H. Davenport is the President's Distinguished Professor in Management and Information Technology at Babson College, a research fellow at the MIT Initiative on the Digital Economy, and a senior adviser at Deloitte Analytics. Author of over a dozen management books, his latest is *Only Humans Need Apply: Winners and Losers in the Age of Smart Machines.*

CHAPTER 10

Understanding Regression Analysis

by Amy Gallo

One of the most important types of data analysis is **regression**. It is a common approach used to draw conclusions from and make predictions based on data, but for those without a statistical or analytical background, it can also be complex and confusing.

To better understand this method and how companies use it, I talked with Thomas Redman, author of *Data Driven: Profiting from Your Most Important Business Asset*. He also advises organizations on their data and data quality programs.

Adapted from "A Refresher on Regression Analysis" on hbr.org, November 4, 2015 (product #H02GBP).

What Is Regression Analysis?

Redman offers this example scenario: Suppose you're a sales manager trying to predict next month's numbers. You know that dozens, perhaps even hundreds, of factors from the weather to a competitor's promotion to the rumor of a new and improved model can impact the number. Perhaps people in your organization even have a theory about what will have the biggest effect on sales. "Trust me. The more rain we have, the more we sell." "Six weeks after the competitor's promotion, sales jump."

Regression analysis is a way of mathematically sorting out which of those variables do indeed have an impact. It answers the questions: Which factors matter most? Which can we ignore? How do those factors interact with one another? And, perhaps most importantly, how certain are we about all of these factors?

In regression analysis, those factors are called variables. You have your **dependent variable**—the main factor that you're trying to understand or predict. In Redman's example above, the dependent variable is monthly sales. And then you have your **independent variables**—the factors you suspect have an impact on your dependent variable.

How Does It Work?

In order to conduct a regression analysis, you gather data on the variables in question. You take all of your monthly sales numbers for, say, the past three years and any data on the independent variables you're interested in. So, in this case, let's say you find out the average monthly rainfall for the past three years as well. Then you plot all of that information on a chart that looks like figure 10-1.

The y-axis is the amount of sales (the dependent variable, the thing you're interested in, is always on the y-axis) and the x-axis is the total rainfall. Each dot represents one month's data—how much it rained that month and how many sales you made that same month.

Glancing at this data, you probably notice that sales are higher on days when it rains a lot. That's interesting to know, but by how much? If it rains three inches, do you know how much you'll sell? What about if it rains four inches?

FIGURE 10-1

Is there a relationship between these two variables?

Plotting your data is the first step to figuring that out.

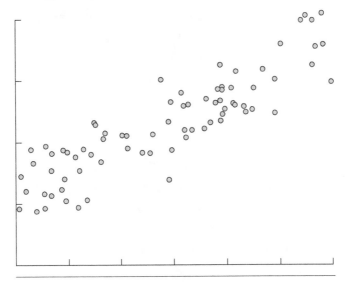

FIGURE 10-2

Building a regression model

The line summarizes the relationship between x and y.

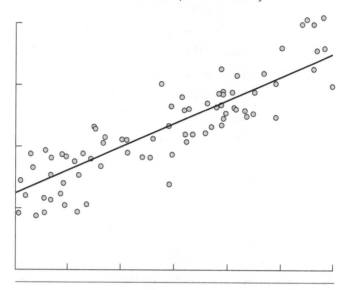

Now imagine drawing a line through the chart, one that runs roughly through the middle of all the data points, as shown in figure 10-2. This line will help you answer, with some degree of certainty, how much you typically sell when it rains a certain amount.

This is called the regression line and it's drawn (using a statistics program like SPSS or STATA or even Excel) to show the line that best fits the data. In other words, explains Redman, "The line is the best explanation of the relationship between the independent variable and dependent variable."

In addition to drawing the line, your statistics program also outputs a formula that explains the slope of the line and looks something like this:

$$y = 200 + 5x + \text{error term}$$

Ignore the error term for now. It refers to the fact that regression isn't perfectly precise. Just focus on the model:

$$y = 200 + 5x$$

What this formula is telling you is that if there is no x then $y = 200$. So, historically, when it didn't rain at all, you made an average of 200 sales and you can expect to do the same going forward assuming other variables stay the same. And in the past, for every additional inch of rain, you made an average of five more sales. "For every increment that x goes up one, y goes up by five," says Redman.

Now let's return to the **error term**. You might be tempted to say that rain has a big impact on sales if for every inch you get five more sales, but whether this variable is worth your attention will depend on the error term. A regression line always has an error term because, in real life, independent variables are never perfect predictors of the dependent variables. Rather, the line is an estimate based on the available data. So the error term tells you how certain you can be about the formula. The larger it is, the less certain the regression line.

This example uses only one variable to predict the factor of interest—in this case, rain to predict sales. Typically, you start a regression analysis wanting to understand the impact of several independent variables. So you might include not just rain but also data about a competitor's promotion. "You keep doing this until the error term is very small," says Redman. "You're trying to get the line that fits best with your data." While there can be dangers in trying to include too many variables in a regression analysis, skilled analysts can minimize those risks. And considering the impact of multiple variables at once is one of the biggest advantages of regression.

How Do Companies Use It?

Regression analysis is the "go-to method in analytics," says Redman. And smart companies use it to make decisions about all sorts of business issues. "As managers, we want to figure out how we can impact sales or employee retention or recruiting the best people. It helps us figure out what we can do."

Most companies use regression analysis to explain a phenomenon they want to understand (why did customer service calls drop last month?); to predict things about the future (what will sales look like over the next six months?); or to decide what to do (should we go with this promotion or a different one?).

Does Correlation Imply Causation?

Whenever you work with regression analysis or any other analysis that tries to explain the impact of one factor on another, you need to remember the important adage: Correlation is not causation. This is critical and here's why: It's easy to say that there is a correlation between rain and monthly sales. The regression shows that they are indeed related. But it's an entirely different thing to say that rain *caused* the sales. Unless you're selling umbrellas, it might be difficult to prove that there is cause and effect.

Sometimes factors are correlated that are obviously not connected by cause and effect, but more often in business it's not so obvious (see the sidebar, "Beware Spurious Correlations," at the end of this chapter). When you see a correlation from a regression analysis, you can't make assumptions, says Redman. Instead, "You have to go out and see what's happening in the real world. What's the physical mechanism that's causing the relationship?" Go out and observe consumers buying your product in the rain, talk to them, and find out what is actually causing them to make the purchase. "A lot of people skip this step and I think it's because they're lazy. The goal is not to figure out what is going on in the data but to figure out what is going on in the world. You have to go out and pound the pavement," he says.

Redman once ran his own experiment and analysis in order to better understand the connection between his travel and weight gain. He noticed that when he traveled, he ate more and exercised less. Was his weight gain caused by travel? Not necessarily. "It was nice to quantify what was happening but travel isn't the cause. It may be related," he says, but it's not like his being on the road put those extra pounds on. He had to understand more about what was happening during his trips. "I'm often in new environments so maybe I'm eating more because I'm nervous." He needed to look more closely at the correlation. And this is his advice to managers. Use the data to guide more experiments, not to make conclusions about cause and effect.

What Mistakes Do People Make When Working with Regression Analysis?

As a consumer of regression analysis, there are several things you need to keep in mind.

First, don't tell your data analyst to go figure out what is affecting sales. "The way most analyses go haywire is the manager hasn't narrowed the focus on what he or she is looking for," says Redman. It's your job to identify the factors that you suspect are having an impact and ask your analyst to look at those. "If you tell a data scientist to go on a fishing expedition, or to tell you something you don't know, then you deserve what you get, which is bad analysis," he says. In other words, don't ask your analysts to look at every variable they can possibly get their hands on all at once. If you do, you're likely to find relationships that don't really exist. It's the same principle as flipping a coin: Do it enough times, you'll eventually *think* you see something interesting, like a bunch of heads all in a row. (For more on how to communicate your data needs to experts, see chapter 4.)

Also keep in mind whether or not you can do anything about the independent variable you're considering. You can't change how much it rains, so how important is it to understand that? "We can't do anything about weather or our competitor's promotion but we can affect our own promotions or add features, for example," says Redman. Always ask yourself what you will do with the data. What actions will you take? What decisions will you make?

Second, "analyses are very sensitive to bad data" so be careful about the data you collect and how you collect it, and know whether you can trust it (as we learned in chapter 8). "All the data doesn't have to be correct or perfect," explains Redman, but consider what you will be doing with the analysis. If the decisions you'll make as a result don't have a huge impact on your business, then it's OK if the data is "kind of leaky." But, "if you're trying to decide whether to build 8 or 10 of something and each one costs $1 million to build, then it's a bigger deal," he says.

Redman also says that some managers who are new to understanding regression analysis make the mistake of ignoring the error term. This is dangerous because they're making the relationship between two variables more certain than it is. "Oftentimes the results spit out of a computer and managers think, 'That's great, let's use this going forward.'" But remember that the results are always uncertain. As Redman points out, "If the regression explains 90% of the relationship, that's great. But if it explains 10%, and you act like it's 90%, that's not good." The point of the analysis is to quantify the certainty that something will happen. "It's not telling you how rain will influence your sales, but it's telling you the probability that rain may influence your sales."

The last mistake that Redman warns against is letting data replace your intuition. "You always have to lay your intuition on top of the data," he explains. Ask yourself whether the results fit with your understanding of the situation. And if you see something that doesn't make sense, ask whether the data was right or whether there is indeed a large error term. Redman suggests you look to more experienced managers or other analyses if you're getting something that doesn't make sense. And, he says, never forget to look beyond the numbers to what's happening outside your office: "You need to pair any analysis with study of the real world. The best scientists—and managers—look at both."

Amy Gallo is a contributing editor at *Harvard Business Review* and the author of the *HBR Guide to Dealing with Conflict*. Follow her on Twitter @amyegallo.

BEWARE SPURIOUS CORRELATIONS

We all know the truism "Correlation doesn't imply causation," but when we see lines sloping together, bars rising together, or points on a scatterplot clustering, the data practically begs us to assign a reason. We want to believe one exists.

Statistically we can't make that leap, however. Charts that show a close correlation are often relying on a visual parlor trick to imply a relationship. Tyler Vigen, a JD student at Harvard Law School and the author of *Spurious Correlations*, has made sport of this on his website, which charts farcical correlations—for example, between U.S. per capita margarine consumption and the divorce rate in Maine.

Vigen has programmed his site so that anyone can find and chart absurd correlations in large data sets. We tried a few of our own and came up with these gems:

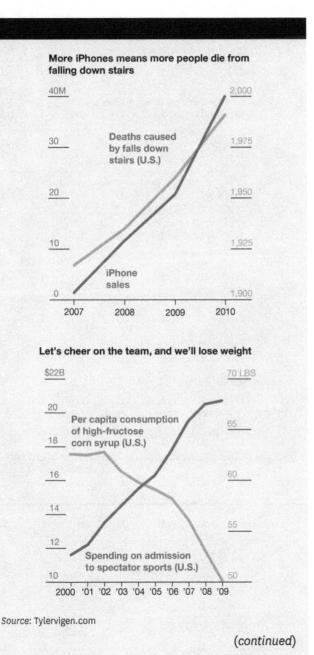

More iPhones means more people die from falling down stairs

40M

2,000

30

Deaths caused
by falls down
stairs (U.S.)

1,975

20

1,950

10

1,925

iPhone
sales

0

1,900

2007 2008 2009 2010

Let's cheer on the team, and we'll lose weight

$22B

70 LBS

20

Per capita consumption
of high-fructose
corn syrup (U.S.)

65

18

16

60

14

55

12

Spending on admission
to spectator sports (U.S.)

50

10

2000 '01 '02 '03 '04 '05 '06 '07 '08 '09

Source: Tylervigen.com

(continued)

BEWARE SPURIOUS CORRELATIONS

(continued)

To increase auto sales, market trips to Universal Orlando

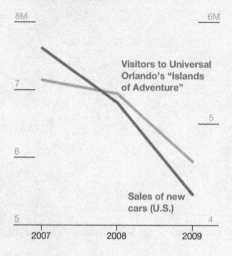

Source: Tylervigen.com

Although it's easy to spot and explain away absurd examples, like these, you're likely to encounter rigged but plausible charts in your daily work. Here are three types to watch out for:

Apples and Oranges: Comparing Dissimilar Variables

Y axis scales that measure different values may show similar curves that shouldn't be paired. This becomes pernicious when the values appear to be related but aren't.

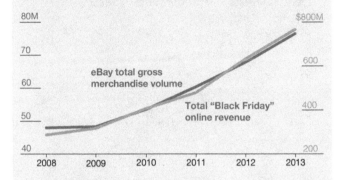

It's best to chart them separately.

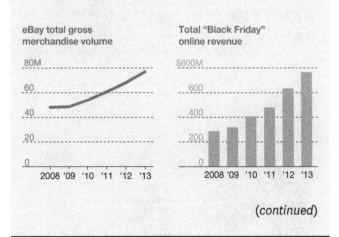

(continued)

BEWARE SPURIOUS CORRELATIONS

(continued)

Skewed Scales: Manipulating Ranges to Align Data

Even when *y* axes measure the same category, changing the scales can alter the lines to suggest a correlation. These *y* axes for RetailCo's monthly revenue difference in range and proportional increase.

Eliminating the second axis shows how skewed this
chart is.

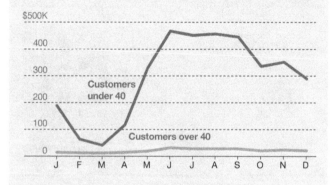

Ifs and *Thens*: Implying Cause and Effect

Plotting unrelated data sets together can make it seem that changes in one variable are causing changes in the other.

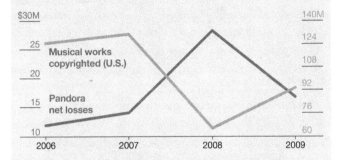

We try to create a narrative—*if* Pandora loses less money, *then* more music is copyrighted—from what is probably a coincidence.

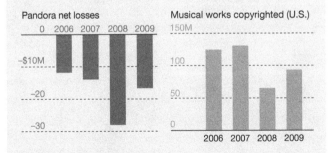

Adapted from "Beware Spurious Correlations," *Harvard Business Review*, June 2015 (product #F1506Z).

CHAPTER 11

When to Act On a Correlation, and When Not To

by David Ritter

"Petabytes allow us to say: 'Correlation is enough.'"

—Chris Anderson,
   Wired, **June 23, 2008**

The sentiment expressed by Chris Anderson in 2008 is a popular meme in the big data community. "Causality is dead," say the priests of analytics and machine learning. They argue that given enough statistical evidence, it's no longer necessary to understand why things happen—we need only know what things happen together.

Adapted from content posted on hbr.org, March 19, 2014 (product #H00Q1X).

But inquiring whether correlation is enough is asking the wrong question. For consumers of big data, the key question is, "Can I take action on the basis of a correlation finding?" The answer to that question is, "It depends"—primarily on two factors:

- **Confidence that the correlation will reliably recur in the future.** The higher that confidence level, the more reasonable it is to take action in response.

- **The trade-off between the risk and reward of acting.** If the risk of acting and being wrong is extremely high, for example, acting on even a strong correlation may be a mistake.

The first factor—the confidence that the correlation will recur—is in turn a function of two things: the frequency with which the correlation has historically occurred (the more often events occur together in real life, the more likely it is that they are connected) and an understanding of what is causing that statistical finding. This second element—what we call "clarity of causality"—stems from the fact that the fewer possible explanations there are for a correlation, the higher the likelihood that the two events are linked. Considering frequency and clarity together yields a more reliable gauge of the overall confidence in the finding than evaluating only one or the other in isolation.

Understanding the interplay between the confidence level and the risk/reward trade-off enables sound decisions on what action—if any—makes sense in light of a particular statistical finding. The bottom line: Causality can matter tremendously. And efforts to gain better insight into the cause of a correlation can drive up the confidence level of taking action.

These concepts allowed The Boston Consulting Group (BCG) to develop a prism through which any potential action can be evaluated. If the value of acting is high, and the cost of acting when wrong is low, it can make sense to act based on even a weak correlation. We choose to look both ways before crossing the street because the cost of looking is low and the potential loss from not looking is high (in statistical jargon what is known as "asymmetric loss function"). Alternatively, if the confidence in the finding is low due to the fact you don't have a handle on why two events are linked, you should be less willing to take actions that have significant potential downside, illustrated in figure 11-1.

FIGURE 11-1

When to act on a correlation in your data

How confident are you in the relationship? And do the benefits of action outweigh the risk?

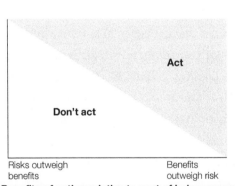

Source: David Ritter, BCG

Consider the case of New York City's sewer sensors. These sensors detect the amount of grease flowing into the sewer system at various locations throughout the city. If the data collected shows a concentration of grease at an unexpected location—perhaps due to an unlicensed restaurant—officials will send a car out to determine the source. The confidence in the meaning of the data from the sensors is on the low side—there may be many other explanations for the excessive influx of grease. But there's little cost if the inspection finds nothing amiss.

Recent decisions around routine PSA screening tests for prostate cancer involved a very different risk/reward trade-off. Confidence that PSA blood tests are a good predictor of cancer is low because the correlation itself is weak—elevated PSA levels are found often in men without prostate cancer. There is also no clear causal explanation for how PSA is related to the development of cancer. In addition, preventative surgery prompted by the test did not increase long-term survival rates. And the risk associated with screening was high, with false positives leading to unnecessary, debilitating treatment. The result: The American Medical Association reversed its previous recommendation that men over 50 have routine PSA blood tests.

Of course, there is usually not just one, but a range of possible actions in response to a statistical finding. This came into play recently in a partnership between an Australian supermarket and an auto insurance company. Combining data from the supermarket's loyalty card program with auto claims information revealed interesting correlations. The data showed that people who buy red meat and milk are good car insurance risks while people who buy pasta and spirits and who fuel their cars at night are poor risks. Though this statistical relationship could be an indicator of risky behaviors (driving under the influence of spirits, for example), there are a number of other possible reasons for the finding.

Potential responses to the finding included:

- Targeting insurance marketing to loyalty card holders in the low-risk group

- Pricing car insurance based on these buying patterns

The latter approach, however, could lead to brand-damaging backlash should the practice be exposed. Looking at the two options via our framework in figure 11-2 makes clear that without additional confidence in the finding, the former approach is preferable.

FIGURE 11-2

If supermarket purchases correlate with auto insurance claims, what should an insurer do?

With the case of relationship unclear, low risk actions are advisible.

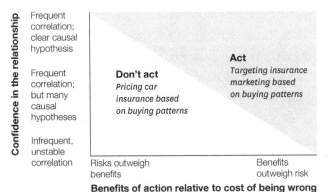

Source: David Ritter, BCG

However, if we are able to find a clear causal explanation for this correlation, we may be able to increase confidence sufficiently to take the riskier, higher-value action of increasing rates. For example, the buying patterns associated with higher risks could be leading indicators of an impending life transition such as loss of employment or a divorce. This possible explanation could be tested by adding additional data to the analysis.

In this case causality is critical. New factors can potentially be identified that create a better understanding of the dynamics at work. The goal is to rule out some possible causes and shed light on what is really driving that correlation. That understanding will increase the overall level of confidence that the correlation will continue in the future—essentially shifting possible actions into the upper portion of the framework. The result may be that previously ruled-out responses are now appropriate. In addition, insight on the cause of a correlation can allow you to look for changes that cause the linkage to weaken or disappear. And that knowledge makes it possible to monitor and respond to events that might make a previously sound response outdated.

There is no shortage of examples where the selection of the right response hinges on this "clarity of cause." The U.S. Army, for example, has developed image processing software that uses flashes of light to locate the possible position of a sniper. But similar flashes also come from a camera. With two potential reasons for the imaging pattern, the confidence in the finding is lower than it would be if there were just one. And that, of course, will determine how to respond—and what level of risk is acceptable.

When working with big data, sometimes correlation is enough. But other times understanding the cause is vital. The key is to know when correlation is enough—and what to do when it is not.

David Ritter is a director in the Technology Advantage practice of The Boston Consulting Group (BCG), where he advises clients on the use of technology for competitive advantage, open innovation, and other topics.

CHAPTER 12

Can Machine Learning Solve Your Business Problem?

by Anastassia Fedyk

As you consider ways to analyze large swaths of data, you may ask yourself how the latest technological tools and automation can help. *AI, big data,* and *machine learning* are all trending buzzwords, but how can you know which problems in your business are amenable to machine learning?

Adapted from "How to Tell If Machine Learning Can Solve Your Business Problem" on hbr.org, November 25, 2016 (product #H03A8R).

To decide, you need to think about the problem to be solved and the available data, and ask questions about feasibility, intuition, and expectations.

Assess Whether Your Problem Requires Learning

Machine learning can help automate your processes, but not all automation problems require learning.

Automation without learning is appropriate when the problem is relatively straightforward—the kinds of tasks where you have a clear, predefined sequence of steps that is currently being executed by a human, but could conceivably be transitioned to a machine. This sort of automation has been happening in businesses for decades. Screening incoming data from an outside data provider for well-defined potential errors is an example of a problem ready for automation. (For example, hedge funds automatically filter out bad data in the form of a negative value for trading volume, which can't be negative.) On the other hand, encoding human language into a structured data set is something that is just a tad too ambitious for a straightforward set of rules.

For the second type of problem, standard automation is not enough. Such complex problems require learning from data—and now we venture into the arena of machine learning. *Machine learning*, at its core, is a set of statistical methods meant to find patterns of predictability in data sets. These methods are great at determining how certain features of the data are related to the outcomes you are interested in. What these methods cannot do is access any knowledge outside of the data you provide. For example, researchers at the University of Pittsburg in the late 1990s evaluated machine-learning algorithms for predicting mortality rates from pneumonia.[1] The algorithms recommended that hospitals send home pneumonia patients who were also asthma sufferers, estimating their risk of death from pneumonia to be lower. It turned out that the data set fed into the algorithms did not account for the fact that asthma sufferers had been immediately sent to intensive care, and had fared better only because of the additional attention.[2]

So what are good business problems for machine learning methods? Essentially, any problems that meet the following two criteria:

1. They require prediction rather than causal inference.

2. They are sufficiently self-contained or relatively insulated from outside influences.

The first means that you are interested in understanding how, on average, certain aspects of the data relate to each other, and not in the causal channels of their relationship. (Keep in mind that the statistical methods do not bring to the table the intuition, theory, or domain knowledge of human analysts.) The second means that you are relatively certain that the data you feed to your learning algorithm includes more or less all there is to the problem. If, in the future, the thing you're trying to predict changes unexpectedly and no longer matches prior patterns in the data, the algorithm will not know what to make of it.

Examples of good machine learning problems include predicting the likelihood that a certain type of user will click on a certain kind of ad, or evaluating the extent to which a piece of text is similar to previous texts you have seen. (To see an example of how an artificial intelligence algorithm learned from existing customer data and test marketing campaigns to find new sales leads, see the sidebar "Artificial Intelligence at Harley-Davidson.")

Bad examples include predicting profits from the introduction of a completely new and revolutionary product line, or extrapolating next year's sales from past data when an important new competitor just entered the market.

ARTIFICIAL INTELLIGENCE AT HARLEY-DAVIDSON

by Brad Power

It was winter in New York City, and Asaf Jacobi's Harley-Davidson dealership was selling one or two motorcycles a week. It wasn't enough.

Jacobi went for a long walk in Riverside Park and happened to bump into Or Shani, CEO of an AI firm, Adgorithms. After discussing Jacobi's sales woes, Shani suggested he try out Albert, Adgorithm's AI-driven marketing platform. It works across digital channels, like Facebook and Google, to measure and then autonomously optimize the outcomes of marketing campaigns. Jacobi decided he'd give Albert a one-weekend audition.

That weekend, Jacobi sold 15 motorcycles—almost twice his all-time summer weekend sales record of eight.

Naturally, Jacobi kept using Albert. His dealership went from getting one qualified lead per day to 40. In the first month, 15% of those new leads were lookalikes, meaning that the people calling the dealership to set up a visit resembled previous high-value customers and therefore were more likely to make a purchase. By the third month, the dealership's leads had increased 2,930%, 50% of them lookalikes, leaving Jacobi scrambling to set up a new call center with six new employees to handle all the new business.

While Jacobi had estimated that only 2% of New York City's population were potential buyers, Albert revealed that his target market was larger—much larger—and began finding customers Jacobi didn't even know existed.

How did it do that?

Albert drove in-store traffic by generating leads, defined as customers who express interest in speaking to a salesperson by filling out a form on the dealership's website. Armed with creative content (headlines and visuals) provided by Harley-Davidson and key performance targets, Albert began by analyzing existing customer data from Jacobi's customer relationship management system to isolate defining characteristics and

(continued)

ARTIFICIAL INTELLIGENCE AT HARLEY-DAVIDSON

(*continued*)

behaviors of high-value past customers: those who either had completed a purchase, added an item to an online cart, viewed website content, or were among the top 25% in terms of time spent on the website.

Using this information, Albert identified lookalikes who resembled these past customers and created micro segments—small sample groups with whom it could run test campaigns before extending its efforts more widely. Albert used the data gathered through these tests to predict which possible headlines and visual combinations, and thousands of other campaign variables, would most likely convert different audience segments through various digital channels (social media, search, display, and email or SMS).

Once it determined what was working and what wasn't, Albert scaled the campaigns, autonomously allocating resources from channel to channel, making content recommendations, and so on.

For example, when it discovered that ads with the word *call*—such as, "Don't miss out on a pre-owned Harley with a great price! Call now!"—performed 447% better than ads containing the word *buy*, such as, "Buy a pre-owned Harley from our store now!" Albert immediately changed *buy* to *call* in all ads across all relevant channels. The results spoke for themselves.

For Harley-Davidson, AI evaluated what was working across digital channels and what wasn't, and used what it learned to create more opportunities for conversion. In other words, the system allocated resources only to what had been proven to work, thereby increasing digital marketing ROI. Using AI, Harley-Davidson was able to eliminate guesswork, gather and analyze enormous volumes of data, and optimally leverage the resulting insights.

Adapted from "How Harley-Davidson Used Artificial Intelligence to Increase New York Sales Leads by 2,930%" on hbr.org, May 30, 2017 (product #H03NFD).

Brad Power is a consultant who helps organizations that must make faster changes to their products, services, and systems to compete with startups and leading software companies.

Find the Appropriate Data

Once you verify that your problem is suitable for machine learning, the next step is to evaluate whether you have the right data to solve it. The data might come from you or from an external provider. In the latter case, ask enough questions to get a good feel for the data's scope and whether it is likely to be a good fit for your problem.

Ask Questions and Look for Mistakes

Once you've determined that your problem is a classic machine learning problem and you have the data to fit it, check your intuition. Machine learning methods, however proprietary and seemingly magical, are statistics. And statistics *can* be explained in intuitive terms.

Instead of trusting that the brilliant proposed method will seamlessly work, ask lots of questions.

Get yourself comfortable with how the method works. Does the intuition of the method roughly make sense? Does it fit conceptually into the framework of the particular setting or problem you are dealing with? What makes this method especially well-suited to your problem? If you are encoding a set of steps, perhaps sequential models or decision trees are a good choice. If you need to separate two classes of outcome, perhaps a binary support vector machine would be best aligned with your needs.

With understanding come more realistic expectations. Once you ask enough questions and receive enough answers to have an intuitive understanding of how the methodology works, you will see that it is far from magical. Every human makes mistakes, and every algorithm is error prone too. For all but the simplest of problems, there *will* be times when things go wrong. The machine learning prediction engine will get things right on average but will reliably make mistakes. And these errors will happen most often in ways that you cannot anticipate.

Decide How to Move Forward

The last step is to evaluate the extent to which you can allow for exceptions or statistical errors in your process. Is your problem the kind where getting things right 80% of the time is enough? Can you deal with a 10% error rate? 5%? 1%? Are there certain kinds of errors that should never be allowed? Be clear and upfront about your needs and expectations, both with yourself and with your solution provider. And once both of you are comfortably on the same page, go ahead. Armed with knowledge, understanding, and reasonable expectations, you are set to reap the benefits of machine learning. Just please be patient.

———————

Anastassia Fedyk is a PhD candidate in business economics at Harvard Business School. Her research focuses on finance and behavioral economics.

NOTES

1. G. F. Cooper et al., "An Evaluation of Machine-Learning Methods for Predicting Pneumonia Mortality," *Artificial Intelligence in Medicine* 9 (1997): 107–138.

2. A. M. Bornstein, "Is Artificial Intelligence Permanently Inscrutable?" *Nautilus*, September 1, 2016, http://nautil.us/issue/40/learning/is-artificial-intelligence-permanently-inscrutable.

CHAPTER 13

A Refresher on Statistical Significance

by Amy Gallo

When you run an experiment or analyze data, you want to know if your findings are significant. But business relevance (that is, practical significance) isn't always the same thing as confidence that a result isn't due purely to chance (that is, statistical significance). This is an important distinction; unfortunately, **statistical significance** is often misunderstood and misused in organizations today. And because more and more companies are relying on data to make critical business decisions, it's an essential concept for managers to understand.

Adapted from content posted on hbr.org, February 16, 2016 (product #H02NMS).

To better understand what statistical significance really means, I talked with Thomas Redman, author of *Data Driven: Profiting from Your Most Important Business Asset*, and adviser to organizations on their data and data quality programs.

What Is Statistical Significance?

"Statistical significance helps quantify whether a result is likely due to chance or to some factor of interest," says Redman. When a finding is significant, it simply means you can feel confident that it's real, not that you just got lucky (or unlucky) in choosing the sample.

When you run an experiment, conduct a survey, take a poll, or analyze a data set, you're taking a sample of some population of interest, not looking at every single data point that you possibly can. Consider the example of a marketing campaign. You've come up with a new concept and you want to see if it works better than your current one. You can't show it to every single target customer, of course, so you choose a sample group.

When you run the results, you find that those who saw the new campaign spent $10.17 on average, more than the $8.41 spent by those who saw the old campaign. This $1.76 might seem like a big—and perhaps important—difference. But in reality you may have been unlucky, drawing a sample of people who do not represent the larger population; in fact, maybe there was no difference between the two campaigns and their influence on consumers' purchasing behaviors. This is called a sampling error, something you must contend with in any test that does not include the entire population of interest.

Redman notes that there are two main contributors to sampling error: the size of the sample and the variation in the underlying population. Sample size may be intuitive enough. Think about flipping a coin 5 times versus flipping it 500 times. The more times you flip, the less likely you'll end up with a great majority of heads. The same is true of statistical significance: With bigger sample sizes, you're less likely to get results that reflect randomness. All else being equal, you'll feel more comfortable in the accuracy of the campaigns' $1.76 difference if you showed the new one to 1,000 people rather than just 25. Of course, showing the campaign to more people costs more money, so you have to balance the need for a larger sample size with your budget.

Variation is a little trickier to understand, but Redman insists that developing a sense for it is critical for all managers who use data. Consider the images in figure 13-1. Each expresses a different possible distribution of customer purchases under campaign A. Looking at the chart on the left (with less variation), most people spend roughly the same amount. Some people spend a few dollars more or less, but if you pick a customer at random, chances are pretty good that they'll be close to the average. So it's less likely that you'll select a sample that looks vastly different from the total population, which means you can be relatively confident in your results.

Compare that with the chart on the right (with more variation). Here, people vary more widely in how much they spend. The average is still the same, but quite a few people spend more or less. If you pick a customer at random, chances are higher that they are pretty far from

FIGURE 13-1

Population variation

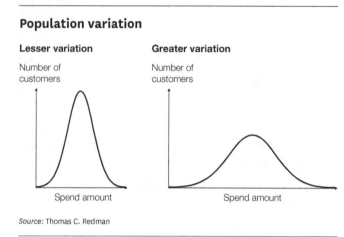

Lesser variation

Number of
customers

Spend amount

Greater variation

Number of
customers

Spend amount

Source: Thomas C. Redman

the average. So if you select a sample from a more varied population, you can't be as confident in your results.

To summarize, the important thing to understand is that the greater the variation in the underlying population, the larger the sampling error.

Redman advises that you should plot your data and make pictures like these when you analyze the numbers. The graphs will help you get a feel for variation, the sampling error, and in turn, the statistical significance.

No matter what you're studying, the process for evaluating significance is the same. You start by stating a null hypothesis. In the experiment about the marketing campaign, the null hypothesis might be, "On average, customers don't prefer our new campaign to the old one." Before you begin, you should also state an alternative hypothesis, such as, "On average, customers prefer the new one," and a target significance level. The significance level is an expression of how rare your results are, under the assumption that the null hypothesis is true. It is usually expressed as a p-value, and the lower the p-value, the less likely the results are due purely to chance.

Setting a target and interpreting p-values can be dauntingly complex. Redman says it depends a lot on what you are analyzing. "If you're searching for the Higgs boson, you probably want an extremely low p-value, maybe 0.00001," he says. "But if you're testing for whether your new marketing concept is better or the new drill bits your engineer designed work faster than your existing bits, then you're probably willing to take a higher value, maybe even as high as 0.25."

Note that in many business experiments, managers skip these two initial steps and don't worry about significance until after the results are in. However, it's good scientific practice to do these two things ahead of time.

Then you collect your data, plot the results, and calculate statistics, including the p-value, which incorporates variation and the sample size. If you get a p-value lower than your target, then you reject the null hypothesis in favor of the alternative. Again, this means the probability is small that your results were due solely to chance.

How Is It Calculated?

As a manager, chances are you won't ever calculate statistical significance yourself. "Most good statistical packages will report the significance along with the results," says Redman. There is also a formula in Microsoft Excel and a number of other online tools that will calculate it for you.

Still, it's helpful to know the process in order to understand and interpret the results. As Redman advises, "Managers should not trust a model they don't understand."

How Do Companies Use It?

Companies use statistical significance to understand how strongly the results of an experiment, survey, or poll they've conducted should influence the decisions they make. For example, if a manager runs a pricing study to understand how best to price a new product, they will calculate the statistical significance (with the help of an analyst, most likely) so that they know whether the findings should affect the final price.

Remember the new marketing campaign that produced a $1.76 boost (more than 20%) in the average sale? It's surely of practical significance. If the p-value comes in at 0.03 the result is also statistically significant, and you should adopt the new campaign. If the p-value comes in at 0.2 the result is not statistically significant, but since the boost is so large you'll probably still proceed, though perhaps with a bit more caution.

But what if the difference were only a few cents? If the p-value comes in at 0.2, you'll stick with your current campaign or explore other options. But even if it had a significance level of 0.03, the result is probably real, though quite small. In this case, your decision probably will be based on other factors, such as the cost of implementing the new campaign.

Closely related to the idea of a significance level is the notion of a confidence interval. Let's take the example of a political poll. Say there are two candidates: A and B. The pollsters conduct an experiment with 1,000 "likely voters." From the sample, 49% say they'll vote for A and 51% say they'll vote for B. The pollsters also report a margin of error of +/- 3%.

"Technically, 49% plus or minus 3% is a 95% confidence interval for the true proportion of A voters in the population," says Redman. Unfortunately, he adds, most people interpret this as "there's a 95% chance that A's true percentage lies between 46% and 52%," but that isn't correct. Instead, it says that if the pollsters were to do the result many times, 95% of intervals constructed this way would contain the true proportion.

If your head is spinning at that last sentence, you're not alone. As Redman says, this interpretation is "maddeningly subtle, too subtle for most managers and even many researchers with advanced degrees." He says the more practical interpretation of this would be "Don't get too excited that B has a lock on the election" or "B appears to have a lead, but it's not a statistically significant one." Of course, the practical interpretation would be very different if 70% of the likely voters said they'd vote for B and the margin of error was 3%.

The reason managers bother with statistical significance is they want to know what findings say about what they should do in the real world. But "confidence intervals and hypothesis tests were designed to support 'science,' where the idea is to learn something that will stand the test of time," says Redman. Even if a finding isn't statistically significant, it may have utility to you and your company. On the other hand, when you're working with large data sets, it's possible to obtain results that are statistically significant but practically meaningless, for example, that a group of customers is 0.000001% more likely to click on campaign A over campaign B. So rather than obsessing about whether your findings are precisely right, think about the implication of each finding for the decision you're hoping to make. What would you do differently if the finding were different?

What Mistakes Do People Make When Working with Statistical Significance?

"Statistical significance is a slippery concept and is often misunderstood," warns Redman. "I don't run into very many situations where managers need to understand it deeply, but they need to know how to not misuse it."

Of course, data scientists don't have a monopoly on the word "significant," and often in businesses it's used to mean whether a finding is strategically important. It's good practice to use language that's as clear as possible when talking about data findings. If you want to discuss whether the finding has implications for your strategy or decisions, it's fine to use the word "significant," but if you want to know whether something is *statistically* significant, be precise in your language. Next time you look at results of a survey or experiment, ask about the statistical significance if the analyst hasn't reported it.

Remember that statistical significance tests help you account for potential sampling errors, but Redman says what is often more worrisome is the non-sampling error: "Non-sampling error involves things where the experimental and/or measurement protocols didn't happen according to plan, such as people lying on the survey, data getting lost, or mistakes being made in the analysis." This is where Redman sees more troubling results. "There is so much that can happen from the time you plan the survey or experiment to the time you get the results. I'm more worried about whether the raw data is trustworthy than how many people they talked to," he says. Clean data and careful analysis are more important than statistical significance.

Always keep in mind the practical application of the finding. And don't get too hung up on setting a strict confidence interval. Redman says there's a bias in scientific literature that "a result wasn't publishable unless it hit a $p = 0.05$ (or less)." But for many decisions—like which marketing approach to use—you'll need a much lower confidence interval. In business, says Redman, there's often more important criteria than statistical significance. The important question is, "Does the result stand up in the market, if only for a brief period of time?"

As Redman says, the results only give you so much information: "I'm all for using statistics, but always wed it with good judgment."

Amy Gallo is a contributing editor at *Harvard Business Review* and the author of the *HBR Guide to Dealing with Conflict*. Follow her on Twitter @amyegallo.

CHAPTER 14

Linear Thinking in a Nonlinear World

by Bart de Langhe, Stefano Puntoni, and Richard Larrick

Test yourself with this word problem: Imagine you're responsible for your company's car fleet. You manage two models, an SUV that gets 10 miles to the gallon and a sedan that gets 20. The fleet has equal numbers of each, and all the cars travel 10,000 miles a year. You have enough capital to replace one model with more-fuel-efficient vehicles to lower operational costs and help meet sustainability goals.

Which upgrade is better?

A. Replacing the 10 MPG vehicles with 20 MPG vehicles

Reprinted from *Harvard Business Review*, May-June 2017 (product #R1703K).

B. Replacing the 20 MPG vehicles with 50 MPG
   vehicles

Intuitively, option B seems more impressive—an increase of 30 MPG is a lot larger than a 10 MPG one.
And the percentage increase is greater, too. But B is not
the better deal. In fact, it's not even close. Let's compare.

Gallons used per 10,000 miles

Current	After upgrade	Savings
A. 1,000 (@10 MPG)	500 (@20 MPG)	500
B. 500 (@20 MPG)	200 (@50 MPG)	300

Is this surprising? For many of us, it is. That's because
in our minds the relationship between MPG and fuel
consumption is simpler than it really is. We tend to think
it's linear and looks like this:

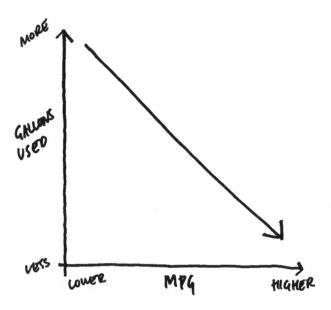

But that graph is incorrect. Gas consumption is not a
linear function of MPG. When you do the math, the relationship actually looks like this:

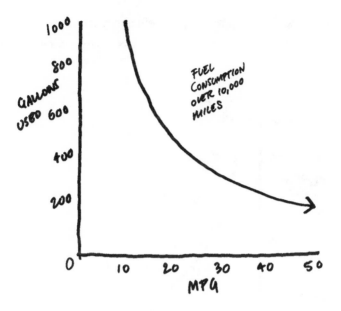

And when you dissect the curve to show each upgrade scenario, it becomes clear how much more effective it is to replace the 10 MPG cars.

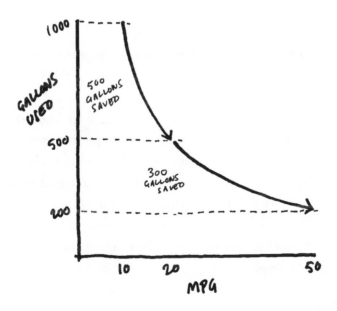

Shockingly, upgrading fuel efficiency from 20 to 100 MPG *still* wouldn't save as much gas as upgrading from 10 to 20 MPG.

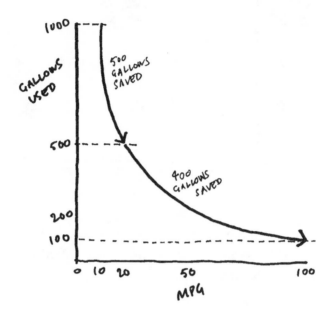

But choosing the lower-mileage upgrade remains counterintuitive, even in the face of the visual evidence. It just doesn't feel right.

If you're still having trouble grasping this, it's not your fault. Decades of research in cognitive psychology show that the human mind struggles to understand nonlinear relationships. Our brain wants to make simple straight lines. In many situations, that kind of thinking serves us well: If you can store 50 books on a shelf, you can store 100 books if you add another shelf, and 150 books if you add yet another. Similarly, if the price of coffee is $2, you can buy five coffees with $10, 10 coffees with $20, and 15 coffees with $30.

But in business there are many highly nonlinear relationships, and we need to recognize when they're in play. This is true for generalists and specialists alike, because even experts who are aware of nonlinearity in their fields can fail to take it into account and default instead to relying on their gut. But when people do that, they often end up making poor decisions.

Linear Bias in Practice

We've seen consumers and companies fall victim to linear bias in numerous real-world scenarios. A common one concerns an important business objective: profits.

Three main factors affect profits: costs, volume, and price. A change in one often requires action on the others to maintain profits. For example, rising costs must be offset by an increase in either price or volume. And if you cut price, lower costs or higher volumes are needed to prevent profits from dipping.

Unfortunately, managers' intuitions about the relationships between these profit levers aren't always good. For years experts have advised companies that changes in price affect profits more than changes in volume or costs. Nevertheless, executives often focus too much on volume and costs instead of getting the price right.

Why? Because the large volume increases they see after reducing prices are very exciting. What people don't realize is just how large those increases need to be to maintain profits, especially when margins are low.

Imagine you manage a brand of paper towels. They sell for 50 cents a roll, and the marginal cost of producing a roll is 15 cents. You recently did two price promotions. Here's how they compare:

	Normal	Promo A: 20% off	Promo B: 40% off
Price/Roll	50¢	40¢	30¢
Sales	1,000	1,200 (+20%)	1,800 (+80%)

Intuitively, B looks more impressive—an 80% increase in volume for a 40% decrease in price seems a lot more profitable than a 20% increase in volume for a 20% cut in price. But you may have guessed by now that B is not the most profitable strategy.

In fact, both promotions decrease profits, but B's negative impact is much bigger than A's. Here are the profits in each scenario:

	Normal	Promo A: 20% off	Promo B: 40% off
Price/Roll	50¢	40¢	30¢
Sales	1,000	1,200 (+20%)	1,800 (+80%)
Profit/Roll	35¢	25¢	15¢
Profit	$350	$300	$270

Although promotion B nearly doubled sales, profits sank almost 25%. To maintain the usual $350 profit during the 40%-off sale, you would have to sell more than 2,300 units, an increase of 133%. The curve looks like this:

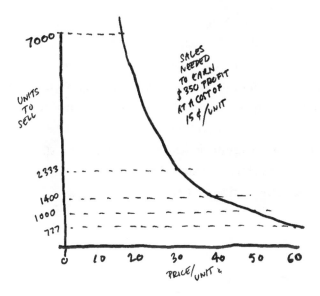

The nonlinear phenomenon also extends to intangibles, like consumer attitudes. Take consumers and sustainability. We frequently hear executives complain that while people say they care about the environment, they are not willing to pay extra for ecofriendly products. Quantitative analyses bear this out. A survey by the National Geographic Society and GlobeScan finds that, across 18 countries, concerns about environmental problems have increased markedly over time, but consumer behavior has changed much more slowly. While nearly all consumers surveyed agree that food production and consumption should be more sustainable, few of them alter their habits to support that goal.

What's going on? It turns out that the relationship between what consumers say they care about and their actions is often highly nonlinear. But managers often believe that classic quantitative tools, like surveys using 1-to-5 scales of importance, will predict behavior in a linear fashion. In reality, research shows little or no behavioral difference between consumers who, on a five-point scale, give their environmental concern the lowest rating, 1, and consumers who rate it a 4. But the difference between 4s and 5s is huge. Behavior maps to attitudes on a curve, not a straight line.

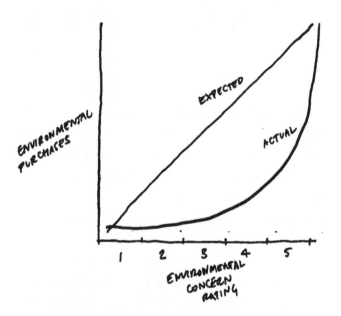

Companies typically fail to account for this pattern—in part because they focus on averages. Averages mask nonlinearity and lead to prediction errors. For example, suppose a firm did a sustainability survey among two of its target segments. All consumers in one segment rate their concern about the environment a 4, while 50% of consumers in the other segment rate it a 3 and 50% rate it a 5. The average level of concern is the same for the two segments, but people in the second segment are overall much more likely to buy green products. That's because a customer scoring 5 is much more likely to make environmental choices than a customer scoring 4, whereas a customer scoring 4 is not more likely to than a customer scoring 3.

The nonlinear relationship between attitudes and behavior shows up repeatedly in important domains, including consumers' privacy concerns. A large-scale survey in the Netherlands, for example, revealed little difference in the number of loyalty-program cards carried by consumers who said they were quite concerned versus only weakly concerned about privacy. How is it possible that people said they were worried about privacy but then agreed to sign up for loyalty programs that require the disclosure of sensitive personal information? Again, because only people who say they are extremely concerned about privacy take significant steps to protect it, while most others, regardless of their concern rating, don't adjust their behavior.

Awareness of nonlinear relationships is also important when choosing performance metrics. For instance, to assess the effectiveness of their inventory management, some firms track days of supply, or the number of days that products are held in inventory, while other firms track the number of times their inventory turns over annually. Most managers don't know why their firm uses one metric and not the other. But the choice may have unintended consequences—for instance, on employee motivation. Assume a firm was able to reduce days of supply from 12 to six and that with additional research, it could further reduce days of supply to four. This is the same as saying that the inventory turn rate could increase from 30 times a year to 60 times a year and that it could be raised again to 90 times a year. But employees are much more motivated to achieve improvements if the firm tracks turnover instead of days of supply, research by the University of Cologne's Tobias Stangl and Ulrich Thonemann shows. That's because they appear to get decreasing returns on their efforts when they improve the days-of-supply metric—but constant returns when they improve the turnover metric.

Other areas where companies can choose different metrics include warehousing (picking time versus picking rate), production (production time versus production rate), and quality control (time between failures versus failure rate).

Nonlinearity is all around us. Let's now explore the forms it takes.

The Four Types of Nonlinear Relationships

The best way to understand nonlinear patterns is to see them. There are four types.

Increasing gradually, then rising more steeply

Say a company has two customer segments that both have annual contribution margins of $100. Segment A has a retention rate of 20% while segment B has one of 60%. Most managers believe that it makes little difference to the bottom line which segment's retention they increase. If anything, most people find doubling the weaker retention rate more appealing than increasing the stronger one by, say, a third.

But customer lifetime value is a nonlinear function of retention rate, as you'll see when you apply the formula for calculating CLV:

$$\frac{\text{Margin} \times \text{Retention Rate}}{1 + \text{Discount Rate} - \text{Retention Rate}}$$

When the retention rate rises from 20% to 40%, CLV goes up about $35 (assuming a discount rate of 10% to adjust future profits to their current worth), but when retention rates rise from 60% to 80%, CLV goes up about $147. As retention rates rise, customer lifetime value increases gradually at first and then suddenly shoots up.

Most companies focus on identifying customers who are most likely to defect and then target them with marketing programs. However, it's usually more profitable to focus on customers who are more likely to stay. Linear thinking leads managers to underestimate the benefits of small increases to high retention rates.

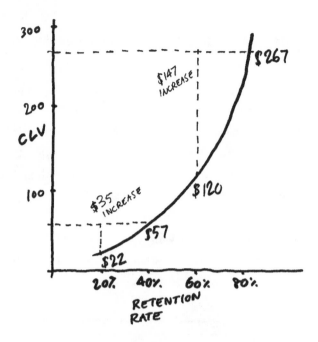

Decreasing gradually, then dropping quickly

The classic example of this can be seen in mortgages. Property owners are often surprised by how slowly they chip away at their debt during the early years of their loan terms. But in a mortgage with a fixed interest rate and fixed term, less of each payment goes toward the principal at the beginning. The principal doesn't decrease linearly. On a 30-year $165,000 loan at a 4.5% interest rate, the balance decreases by only about $15,000 over the first five years. By year 25 the balance will have dropped below $45,000. So the owner will pay off less than 10% of the principal in the first 16% of the loan's term but more than a quarter of it in the last 16%.

Because they're misled by their linear thinking in this context, mortgage payers are often surprised when they

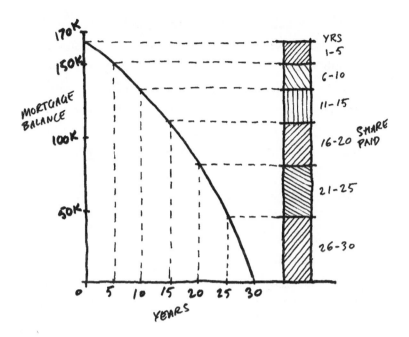

sell a property after a few years (and pay brokerage costs) and have only small net gains to show for it.

Climbing quickly, then tapering off

Selling more of a product allows companies to achieve economies of scale and boost per unit profit, a metric often used to gauge a firm's efficiency. Executives use this formula to calculate per unit profit:

$$\frac{(\text{Volume} \times \text{unit price}) - \text{Fixed Costs} - (\text{Volume} \times \text{Unit Variable Costs})}{\text{Volume}}$$

Say a firm sells 100,000 widgets each year at $2 a widget, and producing those widgets costs $100,000— $50,000 in fixed costs and 50 cents in unit variable costs. The per unit profit is $1. The firm can increase per unit profit by producing and selling more widgets, because it will spread fixed costs over more units. If it doubles the number of widgets sold to 200,000, profit per unit will rise to $1.25 (assuming that unit variable costs remain the same). That attractive increase might tempt you into thinking per unit profit will skyrocket if you increase sales from 100,000 to 800,000 units. Not so.

If the firm doubles widget sales from 400,000 to 800,000 (which is much harder to do than going from 100,000 to 200,000), the per unit profit increases only by about 6 cents.

Managers focus a great deal on the benefits of economies of scale and growth. However, linear thinking may lead them to overestimate volume as a driver of profit and thus underestimate other more impactful drivers, like price.

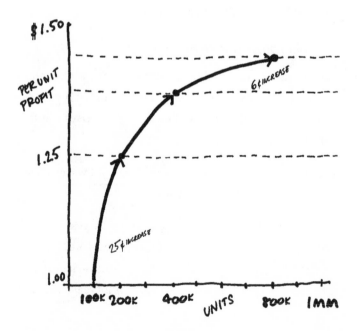

Falling sharply, then gradually

Firms often base evaluations of investments on the payback period, the amount of time required to recover the costs. Obviously, shorter paybacks are more favorable. Say you have two projects slated for funding. Project A has a payback period of two years, and project B has one of four years. Both teams believe they can cut their payback period in half. Many managers may find B more attractive because they'll save two years, double the time they'll save with A.

Company leadership, however, may ultimately care more about return on investment than time to breakeven. A one-year payback has an annual rate of return (ARR) of 100%. A two-year payback yields one of 50%—a 50-point difference. A four-year payback yields one of 25%—a 25-point difference. So as the payback period increases, ARR drops steeply at first and then more slowly. If your focus is achieving a higher ARR, halving the payback period of project A is a better choice.

Managers comparing portfolios of similar-sized projects may also be surprised to learn that the return on investment is higher on one containing a project with a one-year payback and another with a four-year payback than on a portfolio containing two projects expected to pay back in two years. They should be careful not to underestimate the effect that decreases in relatively short payback periods will have on ARR.

How to Limit the Pitfalls of Linear Bias

As long as people are employed as managers, biases that are hardwired into the human brain will affect the quality of business decisions. Nevertheless, it is possible to minimize the pitfalls of linear thinking.

Step 1: Increase awareness of linear bias

MBA programs should explicitly warn future managers about this phenomenon and teach them ways to deal with it. Companies can also undertake initiatives to educate employees by, for instance, presenting them with puzzles that involve nonlinear relationships. In our experience, people find such exercises engaging and eye-opening.

Broader educational efforts are already under way in several fields. One is Ocean Tipping Points, an initiative that aims to make people more sensitive to nonlinear relationships in marine ecosystems. Scientists and managers often assume that the relationship between a stressor (such as fishing) and an ecological response (a decline in fish population) is linear. However, a small change in a stressor sometimes does disproportionately large damage: A fish stock can collapse following a small increase in fishing. The project's goal is to identify relevant tipping points in ocean ecology to help improve the management of natural resources.

Step 2: Focus on outcomes, not indicators

One of senior management's most important tasks is to set the organization's direction and incentives. But frequently, desired outcomes are far removed from everyday business decisions, so firms identify relevant intermediate metrics and create incentives to maximize them. To lift sales, for instance, many companies try to improve their websites' positioning in organic search results.

The problem is, these intermediate metrics can become the end rather than the means, a phenomenon academics call "medium maximization." That bodes trouble if a metric and the outcome don't have a linear relationship—as is the case with organic search position and sales. When a search rank drops, sales decrease quickly at first and then more gradually: The impact on sales is much greater when a site drops from the first to the second position in search results than when it drops from the 20th to the 25th position.

Other times, a single indicator can be used to predict multiple outcomes, and that may confuse people and lead them astray. Take annual rates of return, which a manager who wants to maximize the future value of an investment may consider. If you map the relationship between investment products' ARR and their total accumulated returns, you'll see that as ARR rises, total returns increase gradually and then suddenly shoot up.

Another manager may wish to minimize the time it takes to achieve a particular investment goal. The relationship here is the reverse: As ARR rises, the time it takes to reach a goal drops steeply at first and then declines gradually.

Because ARR is related to multiple outcomes in different nonlinear ways, people often under- or overestimate its effect. A manager who wants to maximize overall returns may care a great deal about a change in the rate from 0.30% to 0.70% but be insensitive to a change from 6.4% to 6.6%. In fact, increasing a low return rate has a much smaller effect on accumulated future returns than increasing a high rate does. In contrast, a manager focused on minimizing the time it takes to reach an investment goal may decide to take on additional risk to increase returns from 6.3% to 6.7% but be insensitive to a change from 0.40% to 0.60%. In this case the effect of increasing a high interest rate on time to completing a savings goal is much smaller than the effect of increasing a low interest rate.

Step 3: Discover the type of nonlinearity you're dealing with

As Thomas Jones and W. Earl Sasser Jr. pointed out in HBR back in 1995 (see "Why Satisfied Customers Defect"), the relationship between customer satisfaction ratings and customer retention is often nonlinear—but in ways that vary according to the industry. In highly competitive industries, such as automobiles, retention rises gradually and then climbs up steeply as satisfaction ratings increase. For noncompetitive industries retention shoots up quickly and then levels off.

In both situations linear thinking will lead to errors. If the industry is competitive, managers will overestimate the benefit of increasing the satisfaction of completely dissatisfied customers. If the industry is not competitive, managers will overestimate the benefit of increasing the satisfaction of already satisfied customers.

The point is that managers should avoid making generalizations about nonlinear relationships across contexts and work to understand the cause and effect in their specific situation.

Field experiments are an increasingly popular way to do this. When designing them, managers should be sure to account for nonlinearity. For instance, many people

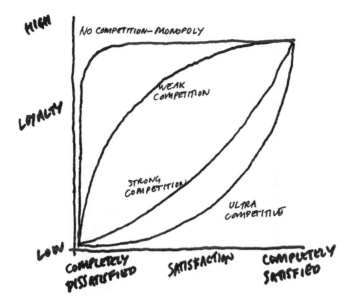

try to measure the impact of price on sales by offering a product at a low price (condition A in the chart on the next page) and a high price (condition B) and then measuring differences in sales. But testing two prices won't reveal nonlinear relationships. You need to use at least three price levels—low, medium (condition C), and high—to get a sense of them.

Step 4: Map nonlinearity whenever you can

In addition to providing the right training, companies can build support systems that warn managers when they might be making bad decisions because of the inclination to think linearly.

Ideally, algorithms and artificial intelligence could identify situations in which that bias is likely to strike and then offer information to counteract it. Of course,

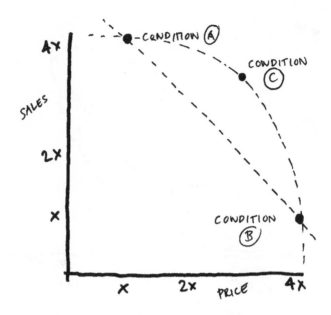

while advances in AI make this possible in formal settings, it can't account for decisions that take place offline and in conversations. And building such systems could eat up a lot of time and money.

A low-tech but highly effective technique for fighting linear bias is data visualization. As you've noticed in this article, whenever we wanted you to understand some linear bias, we showed you the nonlinear relationships. They're much easier to grasp when plotted out in a chart than when described in a list of statistics. A visual representation also helps you see threshold points where outcomes change dramatically and gives you a good sense of the degree of nonlinearity in play.

Putting charts of nonlinear relationships in dashboards and even mapping them out in "what if" scenarios will make managers more familiar with nonlinearity and thus more likely to check for it before making decisions.

Visualization is also a good tool for companies interested in helping customers make good decisions. For example, to make drivers aware of how little time they save by accelerating when they're already traveling at high speed, you could add a visual cue for time savings to car dashboards. One way to do this is with what Eyal Pe'er and Eyal Gamliel call a "paceometer," which shows how many minutes it takes to drive 10 miles. It will surprise most drivers that going from 40 to 65 will save you about six minutes per 10 miles, but going from 65 to 90 saves only about two and a half minutes—even though you're increasing your speed 25 miles per hour in both instances.

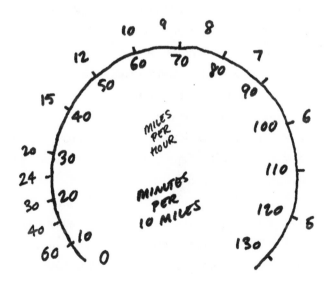

The Implications for Marketers

A cornerstone of modern marketing is the idea that by focusing more on consumer benefits than on product attributes, you can sell more. Apple, for instance, realized that people would perceive an MP3 player that provided "1,000 songs in your pocket" to be more attractive than one with an "internal storage capacity of 5GB."

Our framework, however, highlights the fact that in many situations companies actually profit from promoting attributes rather than benefits. They're taking advantage of consumers' tendency to assume that the relationship between attributes and benefits is linear. And that is not always the case.

We can list any number of instances where showing customers the actual benefits would reveal where they may be overspending and probably change their buying behavior: printer pages per minute, points in loyalty programs, and sun protection factor, to name just a few. Bandwidth upgrades are another good example. Our research shows that internet connections are priced linearly: Consumers pay the same for increases in speed from a low base and from a high base. But the relationship between download speed and download time is nonlinear. As download speed increases, download time drops rapidly at first and then gradually. Upgrading from five to 25 megabits per second will lead to time savings of 21 minutes per gigabyte, while the increase from 25 to 100 Mbps buys only four minutes. When consumers see the actual gains from raising their speed to 100 Mbps, they may prefer a cheaper, slower internet connection.

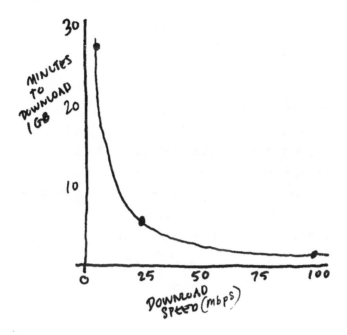

Of course, willfully exploiting consumers' flawed perceptions of attribute-benefit relationships is a questionable marketing strategy. It's widely regarded as unethical for companies to take advantage of customers' ignorance.

In recent years a number of professions, including ecologists, physiologists, and physicians, have begun to routinely factor nonlinear relationships into their decision making. But nonlinearity is just as prevalent in the business world as anywhere else. It's time that management professionals joined these other disciplines in developing greater awareness of the pitfalls of linear thinking in a nonlinear world. This will increase their ability to choose wisely—and to help the people around them make good decisions too.

———————

Bart de Langhe is an associate professor of marketing at Esade Business School, Ramon Llull University, and an assistant professor of marketing at the Leeds School of Business, University of Colorado–Boulder. **Stefano Puntoni** is a professor of marketing at the Rotterdam School of Management, Erasmus University. **Richard Larrick** is the Hanes Corporation Foundation Professor at Duke University's Fuqua School of Business.

CHAPTER 15

Pitfalls of Data-Driven Decisions

by Megan MacGarvie and Kristina McElheran

Even with impressively large data sets, the best analytics tools, and careful statistical methods, managers can still be vulnerable to a range of pitfalls when using data to back up their toughest choices—especially when information overload leads us to take shortcuts in reasoning. In some instances, data and analytics actually make matters worse.

Psychologists, behavioral economists, and other scholars of human behavior have identified several common decision-making traps. Many of these traps stem from the fact that people don't carefully process every piece of information in every decision. Instead, we often rely on *heuristics*—simplified procedures that allow us to make decisions in the face of uncertainty or when extensive analysis is too costly or time-consuming. These heuristics lead us to believe we are making sound decisions when we are actually making systematic mistakes. What's more, human brains are wired for certain biases that creep in and distort our thinking, typically without our awareness.

There are three main cognitive traps that regularly skew decision making, even when informed by the best data. Here are each of these three pitfalls in detail, as well as a number of suggestions for how to escape them.

The Confirmation Trap

When we pay more attention to findings that align with our prior beliefs, and ignore other facts and patterns in the data, we fall into the confirmation trap. With a huge data set and numerous correlations between variables, analyzing all possible correlations is often both costly and counterproductive. Even with smaller data sets, it can be easy to inadvertently focus on correlations that confirm our expectations of how the world should work, and dismiss counterintuitive or inconclusive patterns in the data when they don't align.

Consider the following example: In the late 1960s and early 1970s, researchers conducted one of the most well-designed studies on how different types of fats affect heart health and mortality. But the results of this study, known as the Minnesota Coronary Experiment, were not published at the time. A recent *New York Times* article suggests that these results stayed unpublished for so long because they contradicted the beliefs of both the researchers and the medical establishment.[1] In fact, it wasn't until 2016 that the medical journal *BMJ* published a piece referencing this data, when growing skepticism about the relationship between saturated fat consumption and heart disease led researchers to analyze data from the original experiment—more than 40 years later.[2] These and similar findings cast doubt on decades of unchallenged medical advice to avoid saturated fats. While it's unclear whether one experiment would have changed standard dietary and health recommendations, this example demonstrates that even with the best possible data, when we look at numbers we may ignore important facts when they contradict the dominant paradigm or don't confirm our beliefs, with potentially troublesome results.

This is a sobering prospect for decision makers in companies. And confirmation bias becomes that much harder to avoid when individuals face pressure from bosses and peers. Organizations frequently reward employees who can provide empirical support for existing managerial preferences. Those who decide what parts of the data to examine and present to senior managers may feel compelled to choose only the evidence that reinforces what their supervisors want to see or that confirms a prevalent attitude within the firm.

To get a fair assessment of what the data has to say, don't avoid information that counters your (or your boss's) beliefs. Instead, embrace it by doing the following:

- Specify in advance the data and analytical approaches on which you'll base your decision, to reduce the temptation to cherry-pick findings that agree with your prejudices.

- Actively look for findings that disprove your beliefs. Ask yourself, "If my expectations are wrong, what pattern would I likely see in the data?" Enlist a skeptic to help you. Seek people who like to play devil's advocate or assign contrary positions for active debate.

- Don't automatically dismiss findings that fall below your threshold for statistical or practical significance. Both noisy relationships (those with large standard errors) and small, precisely measured relationships can point to flaws in your beliefs and presumptions. Ask yourself, what would it take for this to appear important? Make sure your key takeaway is not sensitive to reasonable changes in your model or sample size.

- Assign multiple independent teams to analyze the data separately. Do they come to similar conclusions? If not, isolate and study the points of divergence to determine whether the differences are due to error, inconsistent methods, or bias.

- Treat your findings like predictions, and test them. If you uncover a correlation from which you think your organization can profit, use an experiment to validate that correlation.

The Overconfidence Trap

In their book *Judgment in Managerial Decision Making*, behavioral researchers Max Bazerman and Don Moore refer to overconfidence as "The Mother of All Biases." Time and time again, psychologists have found that decision makers are too sure of themselves. We tend to assume that the accuracy of our judgments or the probability of success in our endeavors is more favorable than the data would suggest. When there are risks, we alter our read of the odds to assume we'll come out on the winning side. Senior decision makers who have been promoted based on past successes are especially susceptible to this bias, since they have received positive signals about their decision-making abilities throughout their careers.

Overconfidence also reinforces many other pitfalls of data interpretation, be it psychological or procedural. It prevents us from questioning our methods, motivation, and the way we communicate our findings to others. It makes it easy to underinvest in data and analysis; when we feel too confident in our understanding, we don't spend enough time or money acquiring more information or running further analyses. To make matters worse, more information can increase overconfidence without improving accuracy. More data in and of itself is not a guaranteed solution.

Going from data to insight requires quality inputs, skill, and sound processes. Because it can be so difficult to recognize our own biases, good processes are essential for avoiding overconfidence when analyzing data. Here are a few procedural tips to avoid the overconfidence trap:

- Describe your perfect experiment—the type of information you would use to answer your question if you had limitless resources for data collection and the ability to measure any variable. Compare this ideal with your actual data to understand where it might fall short. Identify places where you might be able to close the gap with more data collection or analytical techniques.

- Make it a formal part of your process to be your own devil's advocate. In *Thinking, Fast and Slow*, Nobel laureate Daniel Kahneman suggests asking yourself why your analysis might be wrong, and recommends that you do this for every analysis you perform. Taking this contrarian view can help you see the flaws in your own arguments and reduce mistakes across the board.

- Before making a decision or launching a project, perform a "pre-mortem," an approach suggested by psychologist Gary Klein. Ask others with knowledge about the project to imagine its failure a year into the future and to write stories of that failure. In doing so, you'll benefit from the wisdom of multiple perspectives, while also providing an opportunity to bring to the surface potential flaws in the analysis that you may otherwise overlook.

- Keep track of your predictions and systematically compare them with what actually happens. Which of your predictions turned out to be true and which ones fell short? Persistent biases can creep back into our decision making; revisit these reports on a regular basis so you can prevent mistakes in the future.

The Overfitting Trap

When your model yields surprising or counterintuitive predictions, you may have made an exciting new discovery—or it may be the result of overfitting. In *The Signal and the Noise*, Nate Silver famously dubbed this "the most important scientific problem you've never heard of." This trap occurs when a statistical model describes random noise, rather than the underlying relationship we need to capture. Overfit models generally do a suspiciously good job of explaining many nuances of what happened in the past, but they have great difficulty predicting the future.

For instance, when Google's Flu Trends application was introduced in 2008, it was heralded as an innovative way to predict flu outbreaks by tracking search terms associated with early flu symptoms. But early versions of the algorithm looked for correlations between flu outbreaks and millions of search terms. With such a large number of terms, some correlations appeared significant when they were really due to chance (searches for "high school basketball," for example, were highly correlated with the flu). The application was ultimately scrapped only a few years later due to failures of prediction.

In order to overcome this bias, you need to discern between the data that matters and the noise around it. Here's how you can guard against the overfitting trap:

- Randomly divide the data into two sets: a training set, with which you'll estimate the model, and a "validation set," with which you'll test the accuracy of the model's predictions. An overfit model might be great at making predictions within the training set, but raise warning flags by performing poorly in the validation set.

- Much like you would for the confirmation trap, specify the relationships you want to test and how you plan to test them *before* analyzing the data, to avoid cherry-picking.

- Keep your analysis simple. Look for relationships that measure important effects related to clear and logical hypotheses before digging into nuances. Be on guard against spurious correlations—the ones that occur only by chance—that you can rule out based on experience or common sense (see the sidebar, "Beware Spurious Correlations," in chapter 10). Remember that data can never truly "speak for itself" and must rely on human interpreters to make sense of it.

- Construct alternative narratives. Is there another story you could tell with the same data? If so, you cannot be confident that the relationship you have uncovered is the right—or only—one.

- Beware of the all-too-human tendency to see patterns in random data. For example, consider a baseball player with a .325 batting average who has no hits in a championship series game. His coach may see a cold streak and want to replace him, but he's only looking at handful of games. Statistically, it would be better to keep him in the lineup than substitute the .200 hitter who had four hits in the previous game.

From Bias to Better Decisions

Data analytics can be an effective tool to promote consistent decisions and shared understanding. It can highlight blind spots in our individual or collective awareness and can offer evidence of risks and benefits for particular paths of action. But it can also make us complacent.

Managers need to be aware of these common decision-making pitfalls and employ sound processes and cognitive strategies to prevent them. It can be difficult to recognize the flaws in your own reasoning—but proactively tackling these biases with the right mindset and procedures can lead to better analysis of data and better decisions overall.

———————

Megan MacGarvie is an associate professor in the markets, public policy, and law group at Boston University's Questrom School of Business, where she teaches data-driven decision making and business analytics.

She is also a research associate of the National Bureau of Economic Research. **Kristina McElheran** is an assistant professor of strategic management at the University of Toronto and a digital fellow at the MIT Initiative on the Digital Economy. Her ongoing work on data-driven decision making with Erik Brynjolfsson has been featured on HBR online and in the *American Economic Review*.

NOTES

1. A. E. Carroll, "A Study on Fats That Doesn't Fit the Story Line," *New York Times*, April 15, 2016.

2. C. E. Ramsden et al., "Re-evaluation of the Traditional Diet-Heart Hypothesis: Analysis of Recovered Data from Minnesota Coronary Experiment (1968-73)," *BMJ* (April 2016), 353:i1246, doi: 10.1136.

CHAPTER 16

Don't Let Your Analytics Cheat the Truth

by Michael Schrage

Everyone's heard the truism that there are lies, damned lies, and statistics. But sitting through a welter of analytics-driven, top-management presentations provokes me into proposing a cynical revision: There are liars, damned liars, and statisticians.

The rise of analytics-informed insight and decision making is welcome. The disingenuous and deceptive manner in which many of these statistics are presented is not. I'm simultaneously stunned and disappointed

---

Adapted from "Do Your Analytics Cheat the Truth?" on hbr.org, October 10, 2011.

by how egregiously manipulative these analytics have become at the very highest levels of enterprise oversight. The only thing more surprising—and more disappointing—is how unwilling or unable so many senior executives are about asking simple questions about the analytics they see.

At one financial services firm, for example, call center analytics showed spike after spike of negative customer satisfaction numbers. Hold times and problem resolution times had noticeably increased. The presenting executive clearly sought greater funding and training for her group. The implied threat was that the firm's reputation for swift and responsive service was at risk.

Three simple but pointed questions later, her analytic gamesmanship became clear. What had been presented as a disturbing customer service trend was in large part due to a policy change affecting about 20% of the firm's newly retired customers. Between their age, possible tax implications, and an approval process requiring coordination with another department, these calls frequently stretched beyond 35 to 45 minutes.

What made the situation worse (and what might explain why the presenter chose not to break out the data) was a management decision not to route those calls to a specially trained team but instead to allow any customer representative to process the query. The additional delays undermined the entire function's performance.

Every single one of the presenter's numbers was technically accurate. But they were aggregated in a manner that made it look as if the function was underresourced. The analytics deliberately concealed the outlier statistically responsible for making the numbers dramatically worse.

More damning was a simple queuing theory simulation demonstrating that if the call center had made even marginal changes in how it chose to manage that exceptional 20%, the aggregate call center performance numbers would have been virtually unaffected. Poor management, not systems underinvestment, was the real root cause problem.

Increasingly, I observe statistical sophisticates indulging in analytic advocacy—that is, the numbers are deployed to influence and win arguments rather than identify underlying dynamics and generate insight. This is particularly disturbing because while the analytics—in the strictest technical sense—accurately portray a situation, they do so in a way that discourages useful inquiry.

I always insist that analytics presentations and presenters explicitly identify the outliers, how they were defined and dealt with, and—most importantly—what the analytics would look like if they didn't exist. It's astonishing what you find when you make the outliers as important as the aggregates and averages in understanding the analytics. (To guide your discussion, consider the questions in the sidebar "Investigating Outliers.")

My favorite example of this comes, naturally enough, from Harvard. Few people realize that, in fact, the average net worth of Harvard dropouts vastly exceeds the average net worth of Harvard graduates.

The reason for that is simple. There are many, many more Harvard graduates than there are Harvard dropouts. But the ranks of Harvard dropouts include Bill by Janice H. Hammond

When you notice an outlier in data, you must investigate why the anomaly exists. Consider asking some of the following questions:

- Is it just an unusual, but valid, value?

- Could it be a data entry error?

- Was it collected in a different way than the rest of the data? At a different time?

After making an effort to understand where an outlier comes from, you should have a deeper understanding of the situation the data represent. Then think about how to handle the outlier in your analysis. Typically, you can do one of three things: leave it alone, or—very rarely—remove it or change it to a corrected value.

Excluding or changing data is not something we do often—and it should be done only after examining the underlying situation in great detail. We should never do it to help the data "fit" a conclusion we want to draw. Changes to a data set should be made on a case-by-case basis only after careful investigation of the situation.

Adapted from "Quantitative Methods Online Course," Harvard Business Publishing, October 24, 2004, revised January 24, 2017 (product #504702).

Janice H. Hammond is the Jesse Philips Professor of Manufacturing at Harvard Business School. She serves as program chair for the HBS Executive Education International Women's Foundation and Women's Leadership Programs, and created the online Business Analytics course for HBX CORe.

Gates, Mark Zuckerberg, and Polaroid's Edwin Land, whose combined, inflation-adjusted net worth probably tops $100 billion. That megarich numerator divided by the smaller "dropout" denominator creates the statistically accurate illusion that the average Harvard dropout is much, much wealthier than the Harvard student who actually got their degree.

This is, of course, ridiculous. Unfortunately, it is no more ridiculous than what one finds, on average, in a statistically significant number of analytics-driven boardroom presentations. The misdirection—and mismanagement—associated with outliers is the most disturbingly common pathology I experience, even in stats-savvy organizations.

Always ask for the outliers. Always make the analysts display what their data looks like with the outliers removed. There are other equally important ways to wring greater utility from aggregated analytics, but start from the outliers in. Because analytics that mishandle outliers are "outliars."

––––––––––

Michael Schrage, a research fellow at MIT Sloan School's Center for Digital Business, is the author of the books *Serious Play, Who Do You Want Your Customers to Become?* and *The Innovator's Hypothesis.*

SECTION FOUR

Communicate Your Findings

CHAPTER 17

Data Is Worthless If You Don't Communicate It

by Thomas H. Davenport

Too many managers are, with the help of their analyst colleagues, simply compiling vast databases of information that never see the light of day, or that only get disseminated in autogenerated business intelligence reports. As a manager, it's not your job to crunch the numbers, but it is your job to communicate them. Never make the mistake of assuming that the results will speak for themselves.

Consider the cautionary tale of Gregor Mendel. Although he discovered the concept of genetic inheritance,

---

Adapted from content posted on hbr.org, June 18, 2013 (product #H00ASW).

his ideas were not adopted during his lifetime because he only published his findings in an obscure Moravian scientific journal, a few reprints of which he mailed to leading scientists. It's said that Darwin, to whom Mendel sent a reprint of his findings, never even cut the pages to read the geneticist's work. Although Mendel carried out his groundbreaking experiments between 1856 and 1863—eight years of painstaking research—their significance was not recognized until the turn of the 20th century, long after his death. The lesson: If you're going to spend the better part of a decade on a research project, also put some time and effort into disseminating your results.

One person who has done this very well is Dr. John Gottman, the well-known marriage scientist at the University of Washington. Gottman, working with a statistical colleague, developed a marriage equation predicting how likely a marriage is to last over the long term. The equation is based on a couple's ratio of positive to negative interactions during a 15-minute conversation on a difficult topic such as money or in-laws. Pairs who showed affection, humor, or happiness while talking about contentious topics were given a maximum number of points, while those who displayed belligerence or contempt received the minimum. Observing several hundred couples, Gottman and his team were able to score couples' interactions and identify the patterns that predict divorce or a happy marriage.

This was great work in itself, but Gottman didn't stop there. He and his wife, Julie, founded a nonprofit research institute and a for-profit organization to apply the results through books, DVDs, workshops, and therapist training. They've influenced exponentially more marriages through these outlets than they could possibly ever have done in their own clinic—or if they'd just issued a press release with their findings.

Similarly, during his tenure at Intuit, George Roumeliotis was head of a data science group that analyzed and created product features based on the vast amount of online data that Intuit collected. For his projects, he recommended a simple framework for communicating about each analysis:

1. My understanding of the business problem

2. How I will measure the business impact

3. What data is available

4. The initial solution hypothesis

5. The solution

6. The business impact of the solution

Note what's not here: details on statistical methods used, regression coefficients, or logarithmic transformations. Most audiences neither understand nor appreciate those details; they care about results and implications. It may be useful to make such information available in an appendix to a report or presentation, but don't let it get in the way of telling a good story with your data— starting with what your audience really needs to know.

Thomas H. Davenport is the President's Distinguished Professor in Management and Information Technology at Babson College, a research fellow at the MIT Initiative on the Digital Economy, and a senior adviser at Deloitte Analytics. Author of over a dozen management books, his latest is *Only Humans Need Apply: Winners and Losers in the Age of Smart Machines.*

CHAPTER 18

When Data Visualization Works—and When It Doesn't

by Jim Stikeleather

I am uncomfortable with the growing emphasis on big data and its stylist, visualization. Don't get me wrong— I love infographic representations of large data sets. The value of representing information concisely and effectively dates back to Florence Nightingale, when she developed a new type of pie chart to clearly show that more soldiers were dying from preventable illnesses than

Adapted from content posted on hbr.org, March 27, 2013 (product #H00ADJ).

from their wounds. On the other hand, I see beautiful exercises in special effects that show off statistical and technical skills, but do not clearly serve an informing purpose. That's what makes me squirm.

Ultimately, data visualization is about communicating an idea that will drive action. Understanding the criteria for information to provide valuable insights and the reasoning behind constructing data visualizations will help you do that with efficiency and impact.

For information to provide valuable insights, it must be interpretable, relevant, and novel. With so much unstructured data today, it is critical that the data being analyzed generates interpretable information. Collecting lots of data without the associated metadata—such as what is it, where was it collected, when, how, and by whom—reduces the opportunity to play with, interpret, and draw conclusions from the data. It must also be relevant to the people who are looking to gain insights, and to the purpose for which the information is being examined (see the sidebar "Understand Your Audience"). Finally, it must be original, or shed new light on an area. If the information fails any one of these criteria, then no visualization can make it valuable. That means that only a tiny slice of the data we can bring to life visually will actually be worth the effort.

Once we've narrowed the universe of data down to that which satisfies these three requirements, we must also understand the legitimate reasons to construct data visualizations, and recognize what factors affect the quality of data visualizations. There are three broad reasons for visualizing data:

- **Confirmation:** If we already have a set of assumptions about how the system we are interested in operates—for example, a market, customers, or competitors—visualizations can help us check those assumptions. They can also enable us to observe whether the underlying system has deviated from the model we had and assess the risk of the actions we are about to undertake based on those assumptions. You see this approach in some enterprise dashboards.

- **Education:** There are two forms of education that visualization offers. One is simply reporting: here is how we measure the underlying system of interest, and here are the values of those measures in some comparative form—for instance, over time, or against other systems or models. The other is to develop intuition and new insights on the behavior of a known system as it evolves and changes over time, so that humans can get an experiential feel of the system in an extremely compressed time frame. You often see this model in the "gamification" of training and development.

- **Exploration:** When we have large sets of data about a system we are interested in and the goal is to provide optimal human-machine interactions (HMI) to that data to tease out relationships, processes, models, etc., we can use visualization to help build a model to allow us to predict and better manage the system. The practice of using visual

UNDERSTAND YOUR AUDIENCE

Before you throw up (pun intended) data in a visualization, start with the goal, which is to convey great quantities of information in a format that is easily assimilated by the consumers of this information—decision makers. A successful visualization is based on the designer understanding whom the visualization is targeting, and executing on three key points:

- Who is the audience, and how will it read and interpret the information? Can you assume these individuals have knowledge of the terminology and concepts you'll use, or do you need to guide them with clues in the visualization (for example, good is indicated with a green arrow going up)? An audience of experts will have different expectations than a general audience.

- What are viewers' expectations, and what type of information is most useful to them?

- What is the visualization's functional role, and how can viewers take action from it? An exploratory visualization should leave viewers with questions to pursue; educational or confirmational graphics should not.

Adapted from "The Three Elements of Successful Data Visualizations" on hbr.org by Jim Stikeleather, April 19, 2013.

discovery in lieu of statistics is called exploratory data analysis (EDA), and too few businesses make use of it.

Assuming the visualization creator has gotten it all right—a well-defined purpose, the necessary and sufficient amount of data and metadata to make the visualization interpretable, enabling relevant and original insights for the business—what gives us confidence that these findings are now worthy of action? Our ability to understand and to a degree control three areas of risk can define the visualization's resulting value to the business:

- **Data quality:** The quality of the underlying data is crucial to the value of visualization. How complete and reliable is it? As with all analytical processes, putting garbage in means getting garbage out.

- **Context:** The point of visualization is to make large amounts of data approachable so we can apply our evolutionarily honed pattern detection computer—our brain—to draw insights from it. To do so, we need to access all of the potential relationships of the data elements. This context is the source of insight. To leave out any contextual information or metadata (or more appropriately, "metacontent") is to risk hampering our understanding.

- **Biases:** The creator of the visualization may influence the visualization's semantics and the syntax of the elements through color choices, positioning, and visual tricks (such as unnecessary 3D, or 2D when 3D is more informative)—any of which can challenge the interpretation of the data. This also creates the risk of pre-specifying discoverable features and results via the embedded algorithms used by the creator (something EDA is intended to overcome). These in turn can significantly influence how viewers understand the visualization, and what insight they will gather from it.

Ignoring these requirements and risks can undermine the visualization's purpose and confuse rather than enlighten.

———————

Jim Stikeleather, DBA, is a serial entrepreneur and was formerly Chief Innovation Officer at Dell. He teaches innovation, business models, strategy, governance, and change management at the graduate level at the University of South Florida and The Innovation Academy at Trinity College Dublin. He is also a senior executive coach.

CHAPTER 19

How to Make Charts That Pop and Persuade

by Nancy Duarte

Displaying data can be a tricky proposition, because different rules apply in different contexts. A sales director presenting financial projections to a group of field representatives wouldn't visualize her data the same way that a design consultant would in a written proposal to a potential client.

So how do you make the right choices for your situation? Before displaying your data, ask yourself these five questions:

Adapted from "The Quick and Dirty on Data Visualization" on hbr.org, April 16, 2014 (product #H00RKA).

1. Am I Presenting or Circulating My Data?

Context plays a huge role in how best to render data. When delivering a presentation, show the conclusions you've drawn, not all the details that led you to those conclusions. Because your slides will be up for only a few seconds, your audience will need to process them quickly. People won't have time to chew on a lot of complex information, and they're not likely to run up to the wall for a closer look at the numbers. Think in broad strokes when you're putting your charts together: What's the overall trend you're highlighting? What's the most striking comparison you're making? These are the sorts of questions to answer with projected data.

Scales, grid lines, tick marks, and such should provide context, but without competing with the data. Use a light neutral color, such as gray, for these elements so they'll recede to the background, and plot your data in a slightly stronger neutral color, such as blue or green. Then use a bright color to emphasize the point you're making.

It's fine to display more detail in documents or in decks that you email rather than present. Readers can study them at their own pace—examine the axes, the legends, the layers—and draw their own conclusions from your body of work. Still, you don't want to overwhelm them, especially since they won't have you there in person to explain what your main points are. Use white space, section heads, and a clear hierarchy of visual elements to help your readers navigate dense content and guide them to key pieces of data.

2. Am I Using the Right Kind of Chart or Table?

When you choose how to visualize your data, you're deciding what type of relationship you want to emphasize. Take a look at figure 19-1, which shows the breakdown of an investment portfolio.

In the pie, it's clear that this person holds a number of investments in different areas—but that's about all you see.

Figure 19-2 shows the same data in a bar chart. In this form it's much easier to discern how much is invested in each category. If your focus is on comparing categories, the bar chart is the better choice. A pie chart would be more useful if you were trying to make the point that a single investment made up a significant portion of the portfolio.

FIGURE 19-1

Investment portfolio breakdown

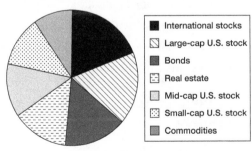

FIGURE 19-2

Investment portfolio breakdown

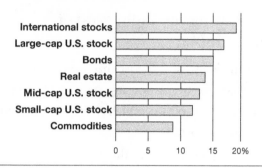

3. What Message Am I Trying to Convey?

Whether you're presenting or circulating your charts, you need to highlight the most important items to ensure that your audience can follow your train of thought and focus on the right elements. For example, figure 19-3 is difficult to interpret because all the information is displayed with equal visual value.

Are we comparing regions? Quarters? Positive versus negative numbers? It's difficult to determine what matters most. By adding color or shading, you can draw the eye to specific areas, as shown in figure 19-4.

We now know that we should be focusing on when and in which regions revenue dropped.

4. Do My Visuals Accurately Reflect the Numbers?

Using a lot of crazy colors, extra labels, and fancy effects won't captivate an audience. That kind of visual clutter

FIGURE 19-3

Revenue trends

	Q1	Q2	Q3	Q4	Total
Americas	−18%	7%	25%	2%	2%
Australia	47%	−7%	26%	15%	17%
China	15%	−5%	1%	7%	19%
Europe	57%	10%	−3%	7%	13%
India	57%	6%	−3%	8%	13%

FIGURE 19-4

Revenue trends

	Q1	Q2	Q3	Q4	Total
Americas	−18%	7%	25%	2%	2%
Australia	47%	−7%	26%	15%	17%
China	15%	−5%	1%	7%	19%
Europe	57%	10%	−3%	7%	13%
India	57%	6%	−3%	8%	13%

dilutes the information and can even misrepresent it. Consider the chart in figure 19-5.

Can you figure out the northern territory's revenue for year one? Is it 17? Or maybe 19? The way some programs create 3D charts would lead any rational person to think that the bar in question is well below 20. However, the data behind the chart actually says that bar represents 20.4 units. You can see that if you look at the chart in a very specific way, but it's difficult to tell which way that should be—even with plenty of time to scrutinize it.

It's much clearer if you simply flatten the chart, as in figure 19-6.

5. Is My Data Memorable?

Even if you've rendered your data clearly and accurately, it's another challenge altogether to make the information stick. Consider using a meaningful visual metaphor to il-

FIGURE 19-5

Yearly revenue per region

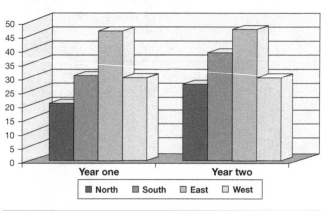

FIGURE 19-6

Yearly revenue per region

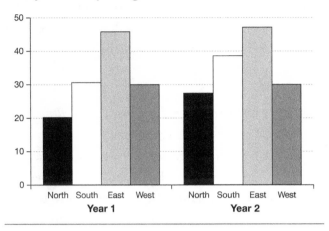

lustrate the scale of your numbers and cement the data in the minds of your audience members. A metaphor can also tie your insights to something that your audience already knows and cares about.

Author and activist Michael Pollan showed how much crude oil goes into making a McDonald's Double Quarter Pounder with Cheese through a striking visual demonstration: He placed glasses on a table and filled them with oil to represent the amount of oil consumed during each stage of the production process. At the end, he took a taste of the oil to drive home his point. (To add an element of humor, he later revealed that his prop "oil" was actually chocolate syrup.)

Pollan could have shown a chart, but this was more effective because he gave the audience a tangible visual— one that triggered a visceral response.

By answering these five questions as you're laying out your data, you'll visualize it in a way that helps people understand and engage with each point in your presentation, document, or deck. As a result, your audience will be more likely to adopt your overall message.

Nancy Duarte has published her latest book, *Illuminate*, with coauthor Patti Sanchez. Duarte is also the author of the *HBR Guide to Persuasive Presentations,* as well as two award-winning books on the art of presenting, *Slide:ology* and *Resonate.* Her team at Duarte Inc. has created more than a quarter million presentations for its clients and teaches public and corporate workshops on presenting. Find Duarte on LinkedIn or follow her on Twitter @nancyduarte.

CHAPTER 20

Why It's So Hard for Us to Communicate Uncertainty

**An interview with Scott Berinato
by Nicole Torres**

We use data to make predictions. But predictions are just educated guesses—they're uncertain. And when they're being communicated, they're incredibly difficult to explain or clearly illustrate.

A case in point: The 2016 U.S. presidential election did not unfold the way so many predicted it would. We now know some of the reasons why—polling failed—but

---

Adapted from "Why It's So Hard for Us to Visualize Uncertainty" on hbr.org, November 11, 2016 (product #H039NV).

watching the real-time results on the night of Tuesday, November 8, wasn't just surprising, it was confusing. Predictions swung back and forth, and it was hard to process the information that was coming in. Not only did the data seem wrong, the way we were presenting that data seemed wrong too.

I asked my colleague Scott Berinato, *Harvard Business Review* editor and author of *Good Charts: The HBR Guide to Making Smarter, More Persuasive Data Visualizations,* if he would help explain this uncertainty— how we dealt with it, why it was so hard to grasp, and what's so challenging about communicating and visualizing it.

Torres: What did you notice about how election predictions were being shown election night?

> **Berinato:** A lot of people were looking at the *New York Times'* live presidential forecast, where you'd see a series of gauges (half-circle gauges, like a gas gauge on your car) that updated frequently.[1] The needle moved left if data showed that Hillary Clinton had a higher chance of winning, and right if Donald Trump did. But the needle also jittered back and forth, making it look like the statistical likelihood of winning was changing rapidly. This caused a lot of anxiety. People were confused. They were trying to interpret what was going on in the election and why the data was changing so drastically in real time, and it was really hard to understand what was going on.
>
> The thing was, the needle wasn't swinging to represent statistical likelihood; it was a hard-coded effect meant to represent uncertainty in the statisti-

cal forecast. So trying to show real-time changes in the race, while accounting for uncertainty, was a good engagement effort, but the execution fell short because it confused and unnerved people. The jitter wasn't the best visual approach.

What do we mean by "uncertainty"?

When thinking about showing uncertainty, we think mostly about two types. One is *statistical uncertainty*, which applies if I said something like, "Here are my values, and statistically my confidence in them is 95%." Think about margin of error built into polls. Statisticians use things like box-and-whisker plots to represent this, where a box shows the upper and lower ranges of the first and third quartiles in a data set, a line in the box marks the median, and thin bar "whiskers" reaching above and below the box to indicate the range of the data. Dots can also be used beyond the whiskers to show outliers. There are lots of variations of these, and they work reasonably well, though academics try other approaches sometimes and the lay audience isn't used to these visualizations, for the most part.

The other kind of uncertainty is *data uncertainty*. This applies when we're not sure where within a range our data falls. Instead of having a value and a confidence in that value, we have a range of possible values. A friend recently gave me a data set with two values. One was "the estimate ranges from 1 in 2,000 to 1 in 4,500" and the other was "an estimate ranging from 1 in 5,500 to 1 in 8,000." There's not an accepted or right way to visualize something like this.

Finding ways to accurately and effectively represent uncertainty is one of the most important challenges in data visualization today. And it's important to know that visualizing uncertainty in general is extremely difficult to do.

Why?

When you think about it, visualizations make something abstract—numbers, statistics—concrete. You are representing an idea like 20% with a thing like a bar or dot. A dot on a line that represents 20% looks pretty certain. How do you then express the idea that "five times out of a hundred this isn't the right answer, and it could be all these other answers"?

So are there good ways of visualizing uncertainty like this?

A lot of the time people just don't represent their uncertainty, because it's hard. We don't want to do that. Uncertainty is an important thing to be able to communicate. For example, consider health care, where outcomes of care may be uncertain but you want people to understand their decisions. How do you show them the possible range of outcomes, instead of only what is the most likely or least likely to happen? Or say there's an outbreak of a disease like Ebola and we want to model the worst case, the most likely, and the best-case scenarios. How do we represent those different outcomes? Weather forecasts, hurricane models are the same thing. Risk analysts and probability experts think about how to solve these problems all the time. It's not easy.

There are a number of other approaches, though. Some people use bars to represent the range of uncertainty. Some use solid lines to show an average value and dotted lines above and below to show the upper and lower boundaries. Using color saturation or gradients to show that values are becoming less and less likely—but still in the realm of possibility—is another way.

On top of uncertainty, we're also dealing with probability.

Yes, it's really hard for our brains to perceive probability. When we say something has an 80% chance of happening, it's not the simplest thing to understand. You can't really feel what 80% likelihood really means. I mean, it seems like it will probably happen. But the important thing to remember is that if it doesn't happen, that doesn't mean you were wrong. It just means the 20% likelihood happened instead.

Statistics are weird. Even if we felt like we understood what a "20% chance" was, we don't think of it as the same as "1 in 5." We tend to think that "1 in 5" is more likely to happen than "20%." It's less abstract. If you say 1 in 5 people commits a crime, you actually picture that one person. We "image the numerator." But "20%" doesn't commit a crime. It's not a thing that acts. It's a statistic.

What do we do when the 20% or 10% chance thing happens?

How do you tell someone who has had the very rare thing happen to them that, based on the probability we gave you, it was the right advice, even though it didn't work out for you? That's really difficult, and security executives and risk experts think about this all the time. When you think about it, businesses need to learn this because it's easy in hindsight to say "Our models were wrong—the unlikely bad thing happened." Not true! We all along were communicating there was some small chance that the bad thing could happen. Still, as humans, that's hard for us to grasp.

Is it because we try to hang on to the hope of a more favorable outcome?

It's because likely things happen more of the time. When unlikely things happen, we want to make sense of it. We weren't expecting it. We shouldn't have been expecting it because it was unlikely. But it's still possible, however unlikely. Already just hearing myself say this, you see how elliptical it sounds. When a natural disaster strikes, you often hear people afterward say "It was a 100-year storm, no one could have seen this coming." Not true! Risk experts always see it coming. It was always a statistical possibility. It's just not likely.

I get probability, but I still can't help but feel misled by the presidential election predictions. What am I missing?

Three things are going on with the election models. (1) Even if a candidate had a 10% chance of winning 10 days ago and they end up winning, it doesn't mean the model was wrong. It means the unlikely happened. (2) This whole notion of using probability to determine who will win an election (based on whether they have an 80% chance, etc.) is hard for the audience to grasp, because we tend to think about elections in more binary terms—this person will win versus that person will win. (3) We revisit the probabilities every day and update them. And when one candidate says something stupid, their probability of winning goes down and the others go up. This makes us feel like these winning probabilities are reactive, not speculative. So we, the lay audience, end up thinking we're looking at data that tells us something about how the candidates are behaving, not how likely it is they'll win. It starts to feel more like an approval rating than a forecast.

That first point must come up in business all the time.

The election brings the subject of visualizing uncertainty into focus but it's an increasingly common challenge in businesses building out their data science operations. As data science becomes more and more important for companies, managers are starting to deal with types of data that show multiple possible outcomes, where there is statistical uncertainty and data uncertainty that they have to communicate to their bosses. If they don't help their bosses understand the uncertainty, they will look at their charts and say that's the answer when it's only the likelihood. It's okay to focus on what is most likely, but you don't want to forgo showing the range of possible outcomes.

For example, if you're looking at a way to model customer adoption and you're using statistical models, you want to make sure you demonstrate what you think is most likely to happen, but also how this outcome is one of a range of potential outcomes based on your models. You need to be able to communicate that visually, or your boss or client will misinterpret what you're saying. If the data scientists say we have a 90% chance of succeeding if we adopt this model, but then it doesn't happen, the boss should know that you weren't wrong—you really just fell into the 10%. You rolled snake eyes. It happens. This is a really hard thing for our brains to deal with and communicate, and it's an important challenge for companies investing in a data-driven approach to their businesses.

Scott Berinato is a senior editor at *Harvard Business Review* and the author of *Good Charts: The HBR Guide to Making Smarter, More Persuasive Data Visualizations* (Harvard Business Review Press, 2016). **Nicole Torres** is an associate editor at *Harvard Business Review*.

NOTE

"Live Presidential Forecast," *New York Times*, November 9, 2016, https://www.nytimes.com/elections/forecast/president.

CHAPTER 21

Responding to Someone Who Challenges Your Data

by Jon M. Jachimowicz

I recently conducted a study with a large, multinational company to figure out how to increase employee engagement. After the data collection was complete, I ran the data analysis and found some intriguing findings that I was excited to share with the firm. But a troubling result became apparent in my analysis: The organization had rampant discrimination against women, especially

---

Adapted from "What to Do When Someone Angrily Challenges Your Data" on hbr.org, April 5, 2017 (product #H03L2M).

ambitious, passionate, talented women. Although this result was based on initial data and was not particularly rigorous, I was convinced that managers at the collaborating organization would like to hear it so that they could address the issue.

I couldn't have been more wrong. In a meeting with the company's head of HR and a few members of his team, I first presented my overall findings about employee engagement. In my last few slides, I turned the presentation toward the results of the gender discrimination analysis that I had conducted. I was expecting an animated conversation, and perhaps even some internal questioning into why the discrimination was occurring and how they could rectify it.

Instead, the head of HR got very angry. He accused me of misrepresenting the facts, and countered by citing data from his own records that showed men and women were equally likely to be promoted. In addition, he had never heard from anyone within the organization that gender discrimination was a problem. He strongly believed that the diversity practices his team had championed were industry leading, and that they were sufficient to ward off gender discrimination. Clearly, this topic was important to him, and my findings had touched a nerve.

After his fury (and my shock) had cooled, I reminded him that the data I presented was just initial pilot data and should be treated as such. Perhaps if we were to do a more thorough assessment, I argued, we would find that the initial data was inaccurate. In addition, I proposed that a follow-on study that focused on gender discrimination could pinpoint which aspects of the diversity policies were working particularly well, and that he could use these insights to further advocate for his agenda. We landed on a compromise: I would design and run an additional study with a focus on gender discrimination, connecting survey responses to important outcomes such as promotions and turnover.

A few months later, the data came in. My data analysis showed that my initial findings were correct: Gender discrimination *was* happening in the company. But the head of HR's major claim wasn't wrong: Men and women were *equally* likely to be promoted.

The improved data set allowed us to see how both facts could be true at the same time. We now had detailed insights into which employees were—and, more important, were *not*—being promoted. Although ambitious, passionate, and talented men were advancing in the company, their female counterparts were being passed over for promotion, time and again—effectively being pushed out of the organization. That is, the best men were moving up, but not the best women. Those women who were being promoted were given these opportunities out of tokenism: They weren't particularly high performing, and often reached a "natural" ceiling early on in their careers due to their limited abilities.

We also now had data on the specific kind of advancement opportunities male and female employees received to learn new skills, make new connections, and increase their visibility in the organization. Compared with their male counterparts, passionate women were less likely to get these kinds of chances.

Armed with this new data, I was invited to present to the head of HR again. Remembering our last meeting, I expected him to be upset. But we had a very different conversation this time. Instead of being met with anger, the data I presented prompted concern. I could place the fact of men and women being equally likely to be promoted in a fuller context, complete with rigorous data from the organization. We had a lively debate about why this asymmetry between men and women existed. Most important, we concluded that the data he measured to track gender discrimination was unable to provide him with the necessary insight to understand whether gender discrimination was a problem.

He has since appointed a task force to tackle the problem of gender discrimination head-on, something he wouldn't have done if we hadn't collected the data that we did. This is the power of collecting thorough data in your own organization: Instead of making assumptions on what may or may not be occurring, a thoughtful design of data-collection practices allows you to gather the right information to come to better conclusions.

So it's not just about the data you have. Existing data blinds us, and it is important to shift the focus away from readily available information. Crucially, not having the right data is no excuse. In the case of the head of HR, not hearing about gender discrimination from anyone in the organization allowed him to conclude that women did not face this issue. Think about what data is *not* being collected that may help embed existing data in a richer context.

Next time someone angrily challenges your data, there are a few steps you can take:

First, take their perspective. Understand why your counterpart is responding so forcefully. In many cases, it may simply be that they really care about the outcome. Your goals may even be aligned, and framing your data in a way where their goals are achieved may help you circumvent their anger.

Second, collect more data that specifically takes their criticism to heart. Every comment is a useful comment. Just as a fiction author can't be upset when readers don't get the point of what they are trying to say, a researcher must understand how their findings are being understood. What is the upset recipient of your analysis responding to, and how can further data collection help you address their concerns?

Last, view your challenger not as an opponent, but as an ally. Find a way to collaborate, because once you have their buy-in, they are invested in the joint investigation. As a result, they will be more likely to view you as being part of the team. And then you can channel the energy that prompted their fury for good.

Defending your data analysis can be stressful—especially if your findings cause conflict. But by following these steps, you can diffuse any tension and attack the problem in a productive way.

Jon M. Jachimowicz is a PhD candidate at Columbia Business School. In his research, he investigates the antecedents, perceptions, and consequences of passion for work. His website can be found at jonmjachimowicz .com.

CHAPTER 22

Decisions Don't Start with Data

by Nick Morgan

I recently worked with an executive keen to persuade his colleagues that their company should drop a longtime vendor in favor of a new one. He knew that members of the executive team opposed the idea (in part because of their well-established relationships with the vendor) but he didn't want to confront them directly, so he put together a PowerPoint presentation full of stats and charts showing the cost savings that might be achieved by the change.

He hoped the data would speak for itself.

But it didn't.

Adapted from content posted on hbr.org, May 14, 2014 (product #H00T3S).

The team stopped listening about a third of the way through the presentation. Why? It was good data. The executive was right. But, even in business meetings, numbers don't ever speak for themselves, no matter how visually appealing the presentation may be.

To influence human decision making, you have to get to the place where decisions are really made—in the unconscious mind, where emotions rule, and data is mostly absent. Yes, even the most savvy executives begin to make choices this way. They get an intent, a desire, or a want in their unconscious minds, and then decide to pursue it and act on that decision. Only after that do they become consciously aware of the choice they've made and start to justify it with rational argument. In fact, research from Carnegie Mellon University indicates that our unconscious minds actually make *better* decisions when left alone to deal with complex issues.

Data is helpful as supporting material, of course. But, because it spurs thinking in the conscious mind, it must be used with care. Effective persuasion starts not with numbers, but with stories that have emotional power because that's the best way to tap into unconscious decision making. We decide to invest in a new company or business line not because the financial model shows it will succeed but because we're drawn to the story told by the people pitching it. We buy goods and services because we believe the stories marketers build around them: "A diamond is forever" (De Beers), "Real beauty" (Dove), "Think different" (Apple), "Just do it" (Nike). We take jobs not only for the pay and benefits but also for the self-advancement story we're told, and tell ourselves, about working at the new place.

Sometimes we describe this as having a good "gut feeling." What that really means is that we've already unconsciously decided to go forward, based on desire, and our conscious mind is seeking some rationale for that otherwise invisible decision.

I advised the executive to scrap his PowerPoint and tell a story about the opportunities for future growth with the new vendor, reframing and trumping the loyalty story the opposition camp was going to tell. And so, in his next attempt, rather than just presenting data, he told his colleagues that they should all be striving toward a new vision for the company, no longer held back by a tether to the past. He began with an alluring description of the future state—improved margins, a cooler, higher-tech product line, and excited customers—then asked his audience to move forward with him to reach that goal. It was a quest story, and it worked.

Data can provide new insight and evidence to inform your toughest decisions. But numbers alone won't convince others. Good stories—with a few key facts woven in—are what attach emotions to your argument, prompt people into unconscious decision making, and ultimately move them to action.

———————

Nick Morgan is a speaker, coach, and the president and founder of Public Words, a communications consulting firm. He is the author of *Power Cues: The Subtle Science of Leading Groups, Persuading Others, and Maximizing Your Personal Impact* (Harvard Business Review Press, 2014).

Data Scientist: The Sexiest Job of the 21st Century

by Thomas H. Davenport and D.J. Patil

When Jonathan Goldman arrived for work in June 2006 at LinkedIn, the business networking site, the place still felt like a startup. The company had just under 8 million accounts, and the number was growing quickly as existing members invited their friends and colleagues to join. But users weren't seeking out connections with the people who were already on the site at the rate executives had expected. Something was apparently missing in the social experience. As one LinkedIn manager put it, "It

---

Reprinted from *Harvard Business Review*, October 2012 (product #R1210D).

was like arriving at a conference reception and realizing you don't know anyone. So you just stand in the corner sipping your drink—and you probably leave early."

Goldman, a PhD in physics from Stanford, was intrigued by the linking he did see going on and by the richness of the user profiles. It all made for messy data and unwieldy analysis, but as he began exploring people's connections, he started to see possibilities. He began forming theories, testing hunches, and finding patterns that allowed him to predict whose networks a given profile would land in. He could imagine that new features capitalizing on the heuristics he was developing might provide value to users. But LinkedIn's engineering team, caught up in the challenges of scaling up the site, seemed uninterested. Some colleagues were openly dismissive of Goldman's ideas. Why would users need LinkedIn to figure out their networks for them? The site already had an address book importer that could pull in all a member's connections.

Luckily, Reid Hoffman, LinkedIn's cofounder and CEO at the time (now its executive chairman), had faith in the power of analytics because of his experiences at PayPal, and he had granted Goldman a high degree of autonomy. For one thing, he had given Goldman a way to circumvent the traditional product release cycle by publishing small modules in the form of ads on the site's most popular pages.

Through one such module, Goldman started to test what would happen if you presented users with names of people they hadn't yet connected with but seemed likely to know—for example, people who had shared their tenures at schools and workplaces. He did this by ginning up a custom ad that displayed the three best new matches for each user based on the background entered in his or her LinkedIn profile. Within days it was obvious that something remarkable was taking place. The click-through rate on those ads was the highest ever seen. Goldman continued to refine how the suggestions were generated, incorporating networking ideas such as "triangle closing"—the notion that if you know Larry and Sue, there's a good chance that Larry and Sue know each other. Goldman and his team also got the action required to respond to a suggestion down to one click.

It didn't take long for LinkedIn's top managers to recognize a good idea and make it a standard feature. That's when things really took off. "People You May Know" ads achieved a click-through rate 30% higher than the rate obtained by other prompts to visit more pages on the site. They generated millions of new page views. Thanks to this one feature, LinkedIn's growth trajectory shifted significantly upward.

A New Breed

Goldman is a good example of a new key player in organizations: the "data scientist." It's a high-ranking professional with the training and curiosity to make discoveries in the world of big data. The title has been around for only a few years. (It was coined in 2008 by one of us, D.J. Patil, and Jeff Hammerbacher, then the respective leads of data and analytics efforts at LinkedIn and Facebook.) But thousands of data scientists are already working at both startups and well-established companies.

Their sudden appearance on the business scene reflects the fact that companies are now wrestling with information that comes in varieties and volumes never encountered before. If your organization stores multiple petabytes of data, if the information most critical to your business resides in forms other than rows and columns of numbers, or if answering your biggest question would involve a "mashup" of several analytical efforts, you've got a big data opportunity.

Much of the current enthusiasm for big data focuses on technologies that make taming it possible, including Hadoop (the most widely used framework for distributed file system processing) and related open-source tools, cloud computing, and data visualization. While those are important breakthroughs, at least as important are the people with the skill set (and the mindset) to put them to good use. On this front, demand has raced ahead of supply. Indeed, the shortage of data scientists is becoming a serious constraint in some sectors. Greylock Partners, an early-stage venture firm that has backed companies such as Facebook, LinkedIn, Palo Alto Networks, and Workday, is worried enough about the tight labor pool that it has built its own specialized recruiting team to channel talent to businesses in its portfolio. "Once they have data," says Dan Portillo, who leads that team, "they really need people who can manage it and find insights in it."

Who Are These People?

If capitalizing on big data depends on hiring scarce data scientists, then the challenge for managers is to learn how to identify that talent, attract it to an enterprise, and make it productive. None of those tasks is as straightforward as it is with other, established organizational roles. Start with the fact that there are no university programs offering degrees in data science. There is also little consensus on where the role fits in an organization, how data scientists can add the most value, and how their performance should be measured.

The first step in filling the need for data scientists, therefore, is to understand what they do in businesses. Then ask, What skills do they need? And what fields are those skills most readily found in?

More than anything, what data scientists do is make discoveries while swimming in data. It's their preferred method of navigating the world around them. At ease in the digital realm, they are able to bring structure to large quantities of formless data and make analysis possible. They identify rich data sources, join them with other, potentially incomplete data sources, and clean the resulting set. In a competitive landscape where challenges keep changing and data never stop flowing, data scientists help decision makers shift from ad hoc analysis to an ongoing conversation with data.

Data scientists realize that they face technical limitations, but they don't allow that to bog down their search for novel solutions. As they make discoveries, they communicate what they've learned and suggest its implications for new business directions. Often they are creative in displaying information visually and making the patterns they find clear and compelling. They advise executives and product managers on the implications of the data for products, processes, and decisions.

Given the nascent state of their trade, it often falls to data scientists to fashion their own tools and even conduct academic-style research. Yahoo, one of the firms that employed a group of data scientists early on, was instrumental in developing Hadoop. Facebook's data team created the language Hive for programming Hadoop projects. Many other data scientists, especially at data-driven companies such as Google, Amazon, Microsoft, Walmart, eBay, LinkedIn, and Twitter, have added to and refined the tool kit.

What kind of person does all this? What abilities make a data scientist successful? Think of him or her as a hybrid of data hacker, analyst, communicator, and trusted adviser. The combination is extremely powerful—and rare.

Data scientists' most basic, universal skill is the ability to write code. This may be less true in five years' time, when many more people will have the title "data scientist" on their business cards. More enduring will be the need for data scientists to communicate in language that all their stakeholders understand—and to demonstrate the special skills involved in storytelling with data, whether verbally, visually, or—ideally—both.

But we would say the dominant trait among data scientists is an intense curiosity—a desire to go beneath the surface of a problem, find the questions at its heart, and distill them into a very clear set of hypotheses that can be tested. This often entails the associative thinking that characterizes the most creative scientists in any field. For example, we know of a data scientist studying a fraud problem who realized that it was analogous to a type of DNA sequencing problem. By bringing together those disparate worlds, he and his team were able to craft a solution that dramatically reduced fraud losses.

Perhaps it's becoming clear why the word "scientist" fits this emerging role. Experimental physicists, for example, also have to design equipment, gather data, conduct multiple experiments, and communicate their results. Thus, companies looking for people who can work with complex data have had good luck recruiting among those with educational and work backgrounds in the physical or social sciences. Some of the best and brightest data scientists are PhDs in esoteric fields like ecology and systems biology. George Roumeliotis, the head of a data science team at Intuit in Silicon Valley, holds a doctorate in astrophysics. A little less surprisingly, many of the data scientists working in business today were formally trained in computer science, math, or economics. They can emerge from any field that has a strong data and computational focus.

It's important to keep that image of the scientist in mind—because the word "data" might easily send a search for talent down the wrong path. As Portillo told us, "The traditional backgrounds of people you saw 10 to 15 years ago just don't cut it these days." A quantitative analyst can be great at analyzing data but not at subduing a mass of unstructured data and getting it into a form in which it can be analyzed. A data management expert might be great at generating and organizing data in structured form but not at turning unstructured data into structured data—and also not at actually analyzing the data. And while people without strong social skills might thrive in traditional data professions, data scientists must have such skills to be effective.

Roumeliotis was clear with us that he doesn't hire on the basis of statistical or analytical capabilities. He begins his search for data scientists by asking candidates if they can develop prototypes in a mainstream programming language such as Java. Roumeliotis seeks both a skill set—a solid foundation in math, statistics, probability, and computer science—and certain habits of mind. He wants people with a feel for business issues and empathy for customers. Then, he says, he builds on all that with on-the-job training and an occasional course in a particular technology.

Several universities are planning to launch data science programs, and existing programs in analytics, such as the Master of Science in Analytics program at North Carolina State, are busy adding big data exercises and coursework. Some companies are also trying to develop their own data scientists. After acquiring the big data firm Greenplum, EMC decided that the availability of data scientists would be a gating factor in its own— and customers'—exploitation of big data. So its Education Services division launched a data science and big data analytics training and certification program. EMC makes the program available to both employees and customers, and some of its graduates are already working on internal big data initiatives.

As educational offerings proliferate, the pipeline of talent should expand. Vendors of big data technologies are also working to make them easier to use. In the meantime one data scientist has come up with a creative approach to closing the gap. The Insight Data Science Fellows Program, a postdoctoral fellowship designed by

HOW TO FIND THE DATA SCIENTISTS YOU NEED

1. Focus recruiting at the "usual suspect" universities (Stanford, MIT, Berkeley, Harvard, Carnegie Mellon) and also at a few others with proven strengths: North Carolina State, UC Santa Cruz, the University of Maryland, the University of Washington, and UT Austin.

2. Scan the membership rolls of user groups devoted to data science tools. The R User Groups (for an open-source statistical tool favored by data scientists) and Python Interest Groups (for PIGgies) are good places to start.

3. Search for data scientists on LinkedIn—they're almost all on there, and you can see if they have the skills you want.

4. Hang out with data scientists at the Strata, Structure:Data, and Hadoop World conferences and similar gatherings (there is almost one a week now) or at informal data scientist "meet-ups" in the Bay Area; Boston; New York; Washington, DC; London; Singapore; and Sydney.

5. Make friends with a local venture capitalist, who is likely to have gotten a variety of big data proposals over the past year.

(continued)

HOW TO FIND THE DATA SCIENTISTS YOU NEED

(continued)

6. Host a competition on Kaggle or TopCoder, the analytics and coding competition sites. Follow up with the most-creative entrants.

7. Don't bother with any candidate who can't code. Coding skills don't have to be at a world-class level but should be good enough to get by. Look for evidence, too, that candidates learn rapidly about new technologies and methods.

8. Make sure a candidate can find a story in a data set and provide a coherent narrative about a key data insight. Test whether he or she can communicate with numbers, visually and verbally.

9. Be wary of candidates who are too detached from the business world. When you ask how their work might apply to your management challenges, are they stuck for answers?

10. Ask candidates about their favorite analysis or insight and how they are keeping their skills sharp. Have they gotten a certificate in the advanced track of Stanford's online Machine Learning course, contributed to open-source projects, or built an online repository of code to share (for example, on GitHub)?

Jake Klamka (a high-energy physicist by training), takes scientists from academia and in six weeks prepares them to succeed as data scientists. The program combines mentoring by data experts from local companies (such as Facebook, Twitter, Google, and LinkedIn) with exposure to actual big data challenges. Originally aiming for 10 fellows, Klamka wound up accepting 30, from an applicant pool numbering more than 200. More organizations are now lining up to participate. "The demand from companies has been phenomenal," Klamka told us. "They just can't get this kind of high-quality talent."

Why Would a Data Scientist Want to Work Here?

Even as the ranks of data scientists swell, competition for top talent will remain fierce. Expect candidates to size up employment opportunities on the basis of how interesting the big data challenges are. As one of them commented, "If we wanted to work with structured data, we'd be on Wall Street." Given that today's most qualified prospects come from nonbusiness backgrounds, hiring managers may need to figure out how to paint an exciting picture of the potential for breakthroughs that their problems offer.

Pay will of course be a factor. A good data scientist will have many doors open to him or her, and salaries will be bid upward. Several data scientists working at startups commented that they'd demanded and got large stock option packages. Even for someone accepting a position for other reasons, compensation signals a level of respect and the value the role is expected to add to the business. But our informal survey of the priorities of data scientists revealed something more fundamentally important. They want to be "on the bridge." The reference is to the 1960s television show *Star Trek*, in which the starship captain James Kirk relies heavily on data supplied by Mr. Spock. Data scientists want to be in the thick of a developing situation, with real-time awareness of the evolving set of choices it presents.

Considering the difficulty of finding and keeping data scientists, one would think that a good strategy would involve hiring them as consultants. Most consulting firms have yet to assemble many of them. Even the largest firms, such as Accenture, Deloitte, and IBM Global Services, are in the early stages of leading big data projects for their clients. The skills of the data scientists they do have on staff are mainly being applied to more-conventional quantitative analysis problems. Offshore analytics services firms, such as Mu Sigma, might be the ones to make the first major inroads with data scientists.

But the data scientists we've spoken with say they want to build things, not just give advice to a decision maker. One described being a consultant as "the dead zone—all you get to do is tell someone else what the analyses say they should do." By creating solutions that work, they can have more impact and leave their marks as pioneers of their profession.

Care and Feeding

Data scientists don't do well on a short leash. They should have the freedom to experiment and explore possibilities. That said, they need close relationships with the rest of the business. The most important ties for them to forge are with executives in charge of products and services rather than with people overseeing business functions. As the story of Jonathan Goldman illustrates, their greatest opportunity to add value is not in creating reports or presentations for senior executives but in innovating with customer-facing products and processes.

LinkedIn isn't the only company to use data scientists to generate ideas for products, features, and value-adding services. At Intuit data scientists are asked to develop insights for small-business customers and consumers and report to a new senior vice president of big data, social design, and marketing. GE is already using data science to optimize the service contracts and maintenance intervals for industrial products. Google, of course, uses data scientists to refine its core search and ad-serving algorithms. Zynga uses data scientists to optimize the game experience for both long-term engagement and revenue. Netflix created the well-known Netflix Prize, given to the data science team that developed the best way to improve the company's movie recommendation system. The test-preparation firm Kaplan uses its data scientists to uncover effective learning strategies.

There is, however, a potential downside to having people with sophisticated skills in a fast-evolving field spend their time among general management colleagues. They'll have less interaction with similar specialists, which they need to keep their skills sharp and their tool kit state-of-the-art. Data scientists have to connect with communities of practice, either within large firms or externally. New conferences and informal associations are springing up to support collaboration and technology sharing, and companies should encourage scientists to become involved in them with the understanding that "more water in the harbor floats all boats."

Data scientists tend to be more motivated, too, when more is expected of them. The challenges of accessing and structuring big data sometimes leave little time or energy for sophisticated analytics involving prediction or optimization. Yet if executives make it clear that simple reports are not enough, data scientists will devote more effort to advanced analytics. Big data shouldn't equal "small math."

The Hot Job of the Decade

Hal Varian, the chief economist at Google, is known to have said, "The sexy job in the next 10 years will be statisticians. People think I'm joking, but who would've guessed that computer engineers would've been the sexy job of the 1990s?"

If "sexy" means having rare qualities that are much in demand, data scientists are already there. They are difficult and expensive to hire and, given the very competitive market for their services, difficult to retain. There simply aren't a lot of people with their combination of scientific background and computational and analytical skills.

Data scientists today are akin to Wall Street "quants" of the 1980s and 1990s. In those days people with backgrounds in physics and math streamed to investment banks and hedge funds, where they could devise entirely new algorithms and data strategies. Then a variety of universities developed master's programs in financial engineering, which churned out a second generation of talent that was more accessible to mainstream firms. The pattern was repeated later in the 1990s with search engineers, whose rarefied skills soon came to be taught in computer science programs.

One question raised by this is whether some firms would be wise to wait until that second generation of data scientists emerges, and the candidates are more numerous, less expensive, and easier to vet and assimilate in a business setting. Why not leave the trouble of hunting down and domesticating exotic talent to the big data startups and to firms like GE and Walmart, whose aggressive strategies require them to be at the forefront?

The problem with that reasoning is that the advance of big data shows no signs of slowing. If companies sit out this trend's early days for lack of talent, they risk falling behind as competitors and channel partners gain nearly unassailable advantages. Think of big data as an epic wave gathering now, starting to crest. If you want to catch it, you need people who can surf.

Thomas H. Davenport is the President's Distinguished Professor in Management and Information Technology at Babson College, a research fellow at the MIT Initiative on the Digital Economy, and a senior adviser at Deloitte Analytics. Author of over a dozen management books, his latest is *Only Humans Need Apply: Winners and Losers in the Age of Smart Machines*. **D.J. Patil** was appointed as the first U.S. chief data scientist and has led product development at LinkedIn, eBay, and PayPal. He is the author of *Data Jujitsu: The Art of Turning Data into Product*.

Index

A/B testing, 59–70
  blocking in, 62
  defined, 60
  example of, 65–67
  interpretation of results,
    63–64
  mistakes in, 68–69
  multivariate, 62–63
  origin of, 60
  overview of, 60–63
  real-time optimization, 68
  retesting, 69
  sequential, 62
  uses of, 64–65
Albert (artificial intelligence
    algorithm), 114–117
analytical models, 15, 22–23, 43,
    84–85, 161, 198. *See also*
    data models
analytics-based decision making.
    See data-driven decisions
Anderson, Chris, 103
annual rate of return (ARR), 145,
    147–148
artificial intelligence (AI),
    114–117, 149–150. *See also*
    machine learning

assumptions
  confirming, through visualiza-
    tions, 179
  in predictive analytics, 84–86
asymmetrical loss function, 105
attributes versus benefits, in
    marketing, 152–153
audience
  data presentations and, 175,
    178, 180, 184, 186, 188–189
  understanding your, 180
automation, 112
averages, 138–139

Bank of America, 18–19
bar charts, 185, 186–188
behavior patterns, 84
bias
  cognitive, 156–163
  confirmation, 156–158
  linear, 135–140, 145–151
  overconfidence, 159–161
  overfitting, 161–163
  visualizations and, 181–182
big data, 13–14, 104, 212, 222,
    223

Harvard Business Review

Invaluable insights
always at your fingertips

With an All-Access subscription to
Harvard Business Review, you'll get
so much more than a magazine.

Exclusive online content and tools
you can put to use today

My Library, your personal workspace for sharing,
saving, and organizing HBR.org articles and tools

Unlimited access to more than 4,000 articles in the
Harvard Business Review archive

Subscribe today at hbr.org/subnow

Smart advice and inspiration from a source you trust.

If you enjoyed this book and want more comprehensive guidance on essential professional skills, turn to the HBR Guides Boxed Set. Packed with the practical advice you need to succeed, this seven-volume collection provides smart answers to your most pressing work challenges, from writing more effective emails and delivering persuasive presentations to setting priorities and managing up and across.

Harvard Business Review Guides

Available in paperback or ebook format. Plus, find downloadable tools and templates to help you get started.

- Better Business Writing
- Building Your Business Case
- Buying a Small Business
- Coaching Employees
- Delivering Effective Feedback
- Finance Basics for Managers
- Getting the Mentoring You Need
- Getting the Right Work Done

- Leading Teams
- Making Every Meeting Matter
- Managing Stress at Work
- Managing Up and Across
- Negotiating
- Office Politics
- Persuasive Presentations
- Project Management

HBR.ORG/GUIDES

Buy for your team, clients, or event.
Visit hbr.org/bulksales for quantity discount rates.

Notes

Notes

Notes

Notes

Notes

Notes

Notes

Notes

Notes

Notes

Notes

Notes